Volume 27   Number 2   1999

Discourse Processes

A MULTIDISCIPLINARY JOURNAL

Special Issue:
Meaning Making
Guest Editor:
Timothy Koschmann

Contents

T0346582

The Society for Text and Discourse Officers for 1999

President
Morton Ann Gernsbacher, *University of Wisconsin, Madison*

Past President
Tom Trabasso, *University of Chicago*

Secretary–Treasurer
Roger Kreuz, *The University of Memphis*

Home Web Page
http://www.psyc.memphis.edu/ST&D/ST&D.htm

Editorial Office
Arthur Graesser
Department of Psychology
The University of Memphis
Campus Box 526400
Memphis, TN 38152–6400
E-mail: a-graesser@memphis.edu

Membership Offices

United States and Canada:	*Outside United States and Canada:*
Roger Kreuz	Herre van Oostendorp
Department of Psychology	Department of Psychology
The University of Memphis	Utrecht University
Campus Box 526400	3584 CS Utrecht
Memphis, TN 38152–6400	The Netherlands
E-mail: kreuzrj@cc.memphis.edu	E-mail: oostendorp@fsw.raa.nl

First published 1999 by Lawrence Erlbaum Associates, Inc.

This edition published 2015 by Routledge
2 Park Square, Milton Park Abingdon, Oxon OX14 4RN
711 Third Avenue New York, NY 10017

Routledge is an imprint of the Taylor & Francis Group, an informa business

ISBN 13: 978-0-805-89805-7 (pbk)

ISSN 0163–853X

DISCOURSE PROCESSES, 27(2), 103–117

EDITOR'S INTRODUCTION

The Edge of Many Circles:
Making Meaning of Meaning Making

Timothy Koschmann
Department of Medical Education
School of Medicine
Southern Illinois University

When the blackbird flew out of sight,
It marked the edge
Of one of many circles.
—Wallace Stevens, "Thirteen Ways of Looking at a Blackbird"

This special issue of *Discourse Processes* focuses on the difficult problem of how we, as observers and researchers, can make sense of how collaborating participants develop a shared understanding of both their task and their own participation in it. Or, stated in another way, how can we derive meaning from their emergent and situated meaning making? Meaning making has been studied under a variety of names (e.g., "intersubjectivity," Matusov, 1996; Rommetveit, 1979; "grounding," Clark & Brennan, 1991; "co-construction," Jacoby & Ochs, 1995; "sense making," Crowder, 1996; "convergent conceptual change," Roschelle, 1996; "managing the intermental," O'Connor, 1996), and as Stevens's poem about the blackbird alludes, meaning can be conceptualized on different levels of abstraction and from a variety of perspectives. Our goal here is to attempt to tease apart some of these views while seeking means to bring them together to provide a more fully elaborated picture.

Correspondence and requests for reprints should be sent to Timothy Koschmann, Department of Medical Education, School of Medicine, Southern Illinois University, P.O. Box 19230, Springfield, IL 62794–1217. E-mail: tkoschmann@acm.org

We approached this task by recruiting a group of researchers with different interests and backgrounds to study and comment on a single piece of data—a 6-min segment of videotaped interaction. The original group consisted of Carl Frederiksen, Phillip Glenn, Jim Greeno, Rogers Hall, Jay Lemke, and Annemarie Palincsar. All six prepared analyses for a panel entitled, "Science Discourse in a PBL Meeting" at the 1996 Meeting of the American Educational Research Association. Expanded versions of five of these analyses are presented here.

The five analyses provide manifold means of observing, describing, and reflecting on a particular event. The assignment to the participating researchers was to carefully examine the video segment and note which aspects caught their eye as being analytically significant. By agreeing to apply their diverse analytic perspectives to a common object of study, they made it possible to bring the differences in their approaches and research traditions into clearer relief.

THE DATA

The 6-min data segment features a group of 2nd-year medical students and a faculty tutor/coach discussing a clinical case. They are participants in a nontraditional medical school curriculum using a teaching method known as problem-based learning (PBL). The segment opens with one of the students, Betty,[1] offering a hypothesis to account for the patient's symptoms. The medical case they are discussing involves an elderly male patient who complains of having problems with his speech and the use of his right leg. Betty's theory is proposed after a period of self-directed study in which the members of the group have independently researched certain questions that arose in an earlier meeting devoted to exploring this case. Her theory implicates a particular structure in the brain ("the hippocampal region") and a side sequence unfolds in which the students, at the tutor/coach's bidding, seek to fix the structure's location in the brain. Betty then proposes a second theory. Thereafter, the group engages in a concerted attempt to coordinate what is known about the case with respect to the two theories. A transcript of the recorded segment is provided in Appendix B (a key to the transcription conventions is provided in Appendix A). A digitized copy of the video segment can be found on the CD–ROM provided with this issue.

THE ANALYSES

The articles are presented in an order designed to make both the data segment and the five analyses more readily understandable. They begin with two relatively

---

[1]The names used here are fictitious.

detailed and concrete descriptions of the action and then advance to three increasingly more abstract treatments.

The first analysis, by Glenn, Koschmann, and Conlee, provides a useful starting point by presenting some background information on PBL. It then gives a microanalytic description of the data segment, drawing on the methods of conversation analysis (CA). Reflecting the influence of the ethnomethodological tradition in sociology, CA seeks to illuminate the features that lend structure to our day-to-day social interactions. The approach is one that eschews the use of preformulated analytic categories in favor of constructing fine-grained descriptions of how people actually manage these interactions (Psathas, 1995). Such an analysis is designed "to show how the parties are embodying for one another the *relevancies* [italics added] of the interaction and are thereby producing the social structure" (Schegloff, 1991, p. 51). Glenn et al. argue that theorizing is "relevant" in the analyzed segment in the sense in which Schegloff used the word in the preceding quote, and the authors document how the group orients to theorizing as a central organizing activity.

Whereas the Glenn et al. article focuses on organizational aspects of the interaction, the second article, by Frederiksen, produces what might be termed a *cognitive ethnography* of the analyzed segment. Frederiksen has worked for over 2 decades developing techniques for representing the semantic content of spoken discourse, and he analyzes the interaction here on several levels. First, he describes the "procedural macrostructure" of the segment. He views the work of the group as an instantiation of what he terms a *differential diagnosis frame* and decomposes the overarching problem-solving task into a hierarchy of subprocedures and goals. Second, he generates three conceptual graphs to represent the propositional content of three portions of the transcribed segment. He then analyzes the microstructure of the analyzed discourse by tracing the inferential links connecting separate speech turns. Finally, Frederiksen analyzes the contributions of each of the participants to the construction of the conceptual models of the case and the overall problem-solving process.

In the third article, Palincsar offers what she terms a *sociocultural* analysis of the data segment. Unlike the two earlier analyses that attempt, respectively, to closely document the interactional features and propositional content of the segment, Palincsar takes a step back from the data and produces a more abstract description of the interaction. Drawing on the writings of Vygotsky and Bruffee and her own work with middle school science students, she focuses on the complex agendas pursued by the medical students in the analyzed segment. The moment captured in the video record is seen as a particular point in the participants' developmental trajectory toward eventual inclusion in a professional community of practice. The participants are in a transitional state, therefore, simultaneously striving to be something more than mere students but not yet having achieved the status of practitioners. In such a state, issues arise pertaining to what constitutes the "authorized language" (Bourdieu, 1977) and who possesses the cultural capital to use it. Palincsar's analysis raises interesting questions about how the students' developing identities interact with their performance as learners in settings of this type.

Lemke's article, the fourth in the series, also acknowledges the mixed agendas evident in the group's interactions. Like Palincsar, Lemke conducts his analysis on a rather abstract plane. He approaches the task from the perspective of a semiotician, that is, as one concerned with how signs and symbols are related to the things they signify. He posits two possible meaning-making strategies: one categorical and discrete, which he terms *typological*, and the other continuous and graded, which he terms *topological*. He argues that typological distinctions are easily relayed via strictly linguistic means, whereas gesture and other forms of visual representation must often be employed to communicate topological distinctions. He observes that there is a potential tension between the use of the two different strategies for coconstructing a shared understanding. Lemke describes two particular examples of this in the video, namely the attempt by the group early in the segment to establish the location of the hippocampus and their later joint effort to coordinate the evidence of the case with Betty's two theories. He concludes that recognition of this tension has certain implications both for those trying to understand situated meaning making and for those attempting to teach in complex and ill-structured domains such as medicine.

The fifth and final analysis, prepared by Hall, offers an interesting contrast to the Glenn et al. analysis described earlier. Although both are microanalytic studies that focus on the organizing features of the interaction, the analyses are conducted in different ways and serve different analytic goals. Hall seeks to provide a developmental account of the competencies displayed in the video segment. To do so, he sets up a contrast with another situation involving "having a theory," namely a previously published (Ochs, Taylor, Rudolph, & Smith, 1992) description of a dinner table discussion involving a 5-year-old child and his mother. Hall borrows certain analytic structures from the Ochs et al. study and shows how they can be applied to a portion of the segment being analyzed here. He also discusses how the two situations might be considered similar and in what ways they should be considered different. By his analysis, the PBL discussion differs from the dinner table discussion in two important ways: the employment of inscriptional technologies (i.e., the anatomical chart) and the much broader generality of the claims being argued for by the medical students.

Included in the issue are two commentary pieces. The first, by Green and McClelland, uses the notion of the expressive potential of a discourse to make comparisions and interrelate observations across analyses. They argue that each of the analyses is representative not only of a research tradition but also of a distinct research language and, as such, can be analyzed on the basis of the expressive potential of that language. The second discussant piece, by Roschelle, takes a different approach to interrelating the five analyses. Roschelle endeavors to show how each of the analyses can be used to illuminate different aspects of Deweyan inquiry. Taken together, the two commentaries elevate the discussion to a plane once removed from the actual data, each providing a metalevel analytic framework for analyzing the analyses.

MANIFOLD VIEWS OF THE SAME EVENT?

Given our original motivation for undertaking this exercise, it is relevant to ask whether the analyses presented here really offer five different views of the same event. The answer would have to be no. Careful examination of the five analyses reveals marked differences in what served as the figure and was treated as ground. This can be seen on several levels.

First, there were differences with respect to which portions of the video segment the analysts directed their attentions. For example, the subsegment in which the students are called on to locate the hippocampus on the atlas chart (lines 16–68) was glossed over in the analyses prepared by Glenn et al. and Frederiksen. This same subsegment, however, was central to the analyses developed by Lemke (see the Locating the Hippocampus section) and Hall (see the Pursuing the Hippocampus Across Representational Media subsection).

Second, there were figure/ground differences in the modalities of expression that the researchers chose to focus on. Although all five analyses dealt with aspects of the participants' talk, some also emphasized the importance of gesture and representational inscription as resources for meaning making. For example, Lemke describes the use of gesture to express topological distinctions, and Hall (see Distributions Across Modes of Activity section) provides an elaborate description of a hand gesture used by one of the students (Maria) to explicate the location of the hippocampus. Similarly, both Lemke and Hall stress the importance of the presence of the anatomic atlas to the group's discussion.

Schegloff (1995) argued that "the absence of actions can be as decisive as their occurrence for the deployment of language and the interactional construction of discourse" (p. 186). A third type of difference, therefore, hinges on whether the analysts included alternative possibilities for action as a substantive component within their analyses. For example, Glenn et al. observe: "The group members orient to theory presentation not only by what they do but also by what they do not do" (p. 130). They cite the silence of other group members during Betty's extended pause in the midst of presenting her first theory as evidence that the group is "orienting to her announced-but-not-yet-presented theory" (p. 123).

As a consequence, even though an effort was made to engage the researchers in the joint analysis of a single event, the analyses differed not only in their treatment of that event but, in each case, in what constituted the event itself. Indeed, this would have likely been the case regardless of how carefully we constrained the data to be analyzed—differences in analytic interests and research questions will inevitably cause each analyst to direct his or her analytic gaze in unique ways. Furthermore, the number of things that can be analyzed in a 6-min segment of video is, for all practical purposes, unlimited. What this suggests, therefore, is that our original goal of specifying a "common event" for analysis may simply not be realizable.

This in no way detracts from the usefulness of this collection, however. In fact, its value arises from its diversity. Pieced together, these five analyses provide us with a much richer understanding of the 6-min segment than could ever be achieved through the application of any particular analytic framework. Actually, this should not come as a surprise. Meaning making is an inherently collaborative undertaking; what we have come to understand here is that the task of making meaning of meaning making must be approached in the same way if we are to make any substantive progress.

REFERENCES

Bourdieu, P. (1977). The economics of linguistic exchanges. *Information sur les Sciences Sociales, 16*, 645–668.

Clark, H., & Brennan, S. (1991). Grounding in communication. In L. Resnick, J. Levine, & S. Teasley (Eds.), *Perspectives on socially-shared cognition* (pp. 127–149). Washington, DC: American Psychological Association.

Crowder, E. (1996). Gestures at work in sense-making science talk. *The Journal of the Learning Sciences, 5*, 173–208.

Jacoby, S., & Ochs, E. (1995). Co-construction: An introduction. *Research on Language and Social Interaction, 28*, 171–184.

Jefferson, G. (1984). Transcription notation. In J. Atkinson & J. Heritage (Eds.), *Structures of social action* (pp. ix–xvi). New York: Cambridge University Press.

Matusov, E. (1996). Intersubjectivity without agreement. *Mind, Culture, and Activity, 3*, 25–45.

Ochs, E., Taylor, C., Rudolph, D., & Smith, R. (1992). Storytelling as a theory-building activity. *Discourse Processes, 15*, 37–72.

O'Connor, M. C. (1996). Managing the intermental: Classroom group discussion and the social context of learning. In D. I. Slobin, J. Gerhardt, A. Kyratzis, & J. Guo (Eds.), *Social interaction, social context, and language: Essays in honor of Susan Ervin-Tripp* (pp. 495–509). Mahwah, NJ: Lawrence Erlbaum Associates, Inc.

Psathas, G. (1995). *Conversation analysis: The study of talk-in-interaction.* Thousand Oaks, CA: Sage.

Rommetveit, R. (1979). On the architecture of intersubjectivity. In R. Rommetveit & R. M. Blaker (Eds.), *Studies of language, thought, and verbal communication* (pp. 93–107). New York: Academic.

Roschelle, J. (1996). Learning by collaboration: Convergent conceptual change. In T. Koschmann (Ed.), *CSCL: Theory and practice of an emerging paradigm* (pp. 209–248). Mahwah, NJ: Lawrence Erlbaum Associates, Inc.

Schegloff, E. (1991). Reflections on talk and social structure. In D. Boden & D. Zimmerman (Eds.), *Talk and social structure* (pp. 44–70). Berkeley: University of California Press.

Schegloff, E. (1995). Discourse as an interactional achievement: III. The omnirelevance of action. *Research on Language and Social Interaction, 28*, 185–212.

APPENDIX A
Transcription Conventions

The notational scheme employed in the data was originally developed by Jefferson (1984). All symbols used in the representation of the data are defined in Table A1.

TABLE A1
Transcription Conventions Used in Appendix B

Symbol	Name	Function
[ ]	Brackets	Marks the beginning and end of overlapping utterances
=	Equal sign	Indicates the end and beginning of two "latched" utterances that continue without a pause
(1.8)	Timed pause	Measured in seconds, this symbol indicates intervals of silence occurring within and between same or different speaker's utterances
(.)	Micropause	A brief pause of less than (0.2)
.	Period	Indicates a falling pitch or intonation
?	Question mark	Rising vocal pitch or intonation
,	Comma	Indicates a continuing intonation, with slight upward or downward contour
-	Hyphen	An abrupt halt of sound, syllable, or word
< >	Greater than/less than signs	Portions of an utterance delivered at a noticeably quicker (> <) or slower (< >) pace than surrounding talk
> <		
°°	Degree signs	Marks texts spoken at a lower volume than surrounding talk
CAPITAL	Capitalized text	Represents speech delivered more loudly than surrounding talk
__	Underscore	Underlined word or syllable indicates stress
↑↓	Arrows	Marks a rise or fall in intonation
:::	Colon(s)	Prolongation of previously indicated sound, syllable, or word
(hhh)		Audible exhalation (linguistic aspiration)
(.hhh)		Audible inhalation
( )	Parentheses	Spoken text in which the transcription is in doubt
(( ))	Double parentheses	Annotations describing nonverbal aspects of the interaction (text italicized)

APPENDIX B
Transcript of the Segment

Segment: My Theory
Tape: 91–002 (0:20:12:20–0:26:10:00)

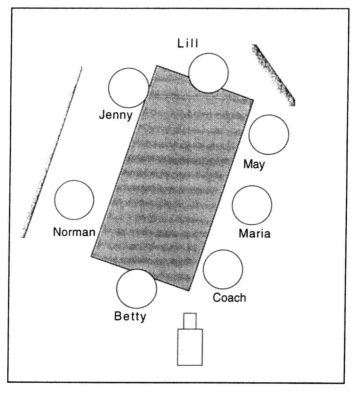

```
 1  |0:20:12:20|   Betty:   See, what it said in here n-my theory
 2                          ┌about this
 3  |0:20:15:00|   (?):     └khu-(.hhhh)
 4  |0:20:15:00|   Betty:   amnesic (.) dysnomic aphasia? (0.6) um it
 5                          says the cause of lesion is usually deep
 6                          in temporal lobe just like Maria was
 7                          saying presumably interrupting
 8                          connections of sensory speech areas with
 9                          the hippocampal and parahippocampal
10                          regions. (1.0)
11                          and I think the hippocampus
12                          is like a lot more medial so if it was
13                          affecting that area it might be the
```

```
14                               ┌anterior cerebral circulation.
15  |0:20:33:00|   Norman:      └Anterior.
16  |0:20:35:00|   Coach:       Where is the hippocampus.
17  |0:20:37:00|   Betty:       I don-do we have a picture up there
18                               on ┌the
19  |0:20:38:00|   Norman:      It'└s right down there, it's the bottom of
20                               this thing.
21                               (2.5) ((Walks over to chart, points))
22                               Right in here
23                               (1.2)
24  |0:20:45:00|   Maria:       ┌I think it's un:der that.
25  |0:20:45:00|   (Jenny):     └(I can't remember)
26  |0:20:47:00|   Norman:      It's under that?
27  |0:20:48:00|   Maria:       I think it's on the inside.
28  |0:20:49:00|   Coach:       It's on the middle, (0.7) middle top.
29  |0:20:52:00|   Maria:       Sts-lk-if you lift (("lifting" gesture
30                               with right arm, elbow out)) up that little
31                               temporal lobe, ┌it's on the inside.
32  |0:20:55:00|   Coach:                      └You can you can point to it
33                               on the middle top.
34                               (1.1)
35  |0:20:57:00|   Maria:       Middle top?
36  |0:20:58:00|   Coach:       Mm-mmm.
37                               (1.5)
38  |0:21:01:00|   Maria:       °Ye:ah its,°
39                               (3.5)
40  |0:21:04:00|   Lill:        In here? ((points to chart))=
41  |0:21:05:00|   Maria:       =Yeah, ┌yeah
42  |0:21:05:00|   Norman:             ┝yeah
43  |0:21:06:00|   Coach:              └That's it (0.2) tha:t's the
44                               hippocampus, then you go over one more
45                               gyrus and you're in the temporal lobe.
46  |0:21:10:00|   Maria:       °Ri:ght°
47  |0:21:11:00|   Coach:       So you can also see it on the (0.6)
48                               frontal.
49                               (1.5)
50  |0:21:15:00|   Coach:       No (you can find it) on the second row left
51                               from there
52                               (3.3)
53  |0:21:21:00|   Norman:      (hh hh hh)
```

```
54                           (1.5)
55  |0:21:24:00|   Coach:   Where would it be in that section.
56                           (1.5)
57  |0:21:26:00|   Lill:    °Somewhere in here?° ((pointing))
58                           (1.5)
59  |0:21:29:00|   Coach:   Th:at's white matter.
60                           (2.2)
61  |0:21:31:20|   Maria:   °In that crevice?°
62  |0:21:33:00|   Norman:         └Go to the crevice there.
63                           (1.0)
64  |0:21:34:00|   Norman:  That little loop?
65                           (1.0)
66  |0:21:36:00|   Norman:  Yeah.
67                           (1.0)
68  |0:21:37:00|   Coach:   That's it.
69  |0:21:38:00|   Betty:   My other theory is that if it was- i- i-
70                           if it's not a vascular lesion but a space
71                           occupying lesion if it was (.) right
72                           there ((points to chart)) in the area we
73                           were pointing to it would be like in a
74                           posterior limb of the internal capsule
75                           which would be where (.) the
76                           corticospinals to the leg would be going
77                           through that part.
78                           (1.0)
79  |0:21:53:00|   Maria:   Wouldn't you expect to ┌see a lot=
80  |0:21:53:00|   Norman:             ┌          └(khh hh huh hh)
81  |0:21:53:00|   Coach:   └Whoa ┌kay
82  |0:21:53:00|   Maria:         └greater in┌volvement if you got
83  |0:21:55:00|   Norman:                    └(hh hh)
84  |0:21:58:00|   Norman:  Yeah
85  |0:21:59:00|   Maria:   internal capsule?=
86  |0:22:02:00|   Betty:   =If it's small. >I mean if< it's
87                           in the very posterior li:mb, (.)
88                           posterior part of the posterior
89                           li:mb. (1.0) Because there's a-the-
90                           (2.0) somato:graphic whatever
91                           that word was, (.) arrangement of the
92                           corticospinals as they go
```

```
 93  |0:22:13:00|   (?):    ⌐°right°
 94  |0:22:13:00|  Betty:   Lthrough the (internal) ⌐capsule.
 95  |0:22:14:00|  Norman:                          LYeah
 96  |0:22:16:00|  Betty:   If you get way to the posterior ↑part of
 97                         the internal capsule the only thing
 98                         that's there ⌐is motor and it's
 99  |0:22:18:00|  Norman:               Lmotor
100  |0:22:18:00|  Betty:   going t⌐o be the le:g.
101  |0:22:19:00|  Norman:         Lmotor
102  |0:22:21:00|  Norman:  That's true
103                         (3.0)
104  |0:22:24:00|  Coach:   So why do the leg findings go away?
105                         (1.0)
106  |0:22:27:00|  Betty:   That's a good question that kind of goes
107                         against it being some kind of a space
108                         occupying lesion because you would expect
109                         it to get progressive and then (you want
110                         it) to involve more areas.
111                         (0.4)
112  |0:22:34:00|  Betty:   So then it's ⌐probably more likely
113  |0:22:35:00|  Maria:                LHeadaches,=
114  |0:22:36:00|  Maria:   =you would expect
115  |0:22:36:15|  Norman:  You'd expect to have headaches
116  |0:22:37:00|  Betty:   °Maybe, yeah.°
117  |0:22:38:00|  Maria:   Seizures.
118                         (0.7)
119  |0:22:41:00|  Betty:   Um (0.8) it's more likely to be vascular.
120                         (2.5)
121  |0:22:45:00|  Coach:   °Oka⌐y°
122  |0:22:46:00|  Maria:       L°With his history an⌐d social°
123  |0:22:46:15|  Coach:                           LSo
124  |0:22:48:00|  Coach:   So if it's vascular did he have a ↑stroke
125                         or is he having a TIA. What is the
126                         difference between those two things
127                         anyway.
128  |0:22:53:00|  Norman:  With TIAs, it's like twenty-four
129                         hour⌐s
130  |0:22:55:00|  Jenny:       LTIAs well, a↑ccording to Harrison's TIAs
131                         um shows some neurological damage but
```

```
132                                 it's all better in twenty-four hours.
133                                 According to Cecil's it's all better in
134                                 one hour um a ┌(hh hh hh)
135  |0:23:09:00|     Lill:                      └(one of 'em)
136  |0:23:11:00|     Jenny:   and Cecil's also talked about something
137                                 called RI:ND (.) which is a reversible
138                                 icschemic (1.6)
139                                 ┌neurological deficits?=
140  |0:23:16:00|     Norman:  ├┌neurological deficits
141  |0:23:16:00|     Coach:   └neurological deficits
142  |0:23:19:20|     Jenny:   =which is somewhere in between a
143                                 completed stroke and a TIA. Which, (hh
144                                 huh huh)=
145  |0:23:25:00|     Betty:   Sorta like angina or ┌unstable angina of
146  |0:23:26:00|     Jenny:                        └(hh huh huh huh)
147  |0:23:27:00|     Betty:   the mind.
148  |0:23:29:00|     Jenny:   =which um (.) gets better within twenty-
149                                 four to thirty-↑six hours, um,
150                                 (1.2) ((Lips smack then mouths something
151                                 like "I don't know"))
152  |0:23:38:00|     Coach:   So which one did he ha:ve?
153                                 (1.0)
154  |0:23:40:00|     Jenny:   °Mm.°
155  |0:23:41:00|     Maria:   I think he's ┌(.) progressing to a
156  |0:23:41:10|     Norman:                └>A little bit of both.<
157  |0:23:43:00|     Maria:   stroke.
158  |0:23:43:20|     Betty:   I think it's really hard to say because I
159                                 don't think we have a very good history
160                                 ↓about exactly what's happened in the
161                                 last three weeks. And I don't know how
162                                 we can im↑prove that.
163  |0:23:50:00|     Jenny:   We don't know how long his ↓leg was
164                                 clumsy
165                                 (0.5)
166  |0:23:53:00|     Betty:   The leg was ┌(clum)
167  |0:23:54:00|     Norman:               └We don't know how long it was
168                                 clumsy? It's gone now yet he still has
169                                 the ↑verbal problem.
170                                 (1.5)
```

```
171  |0:23:59:00|  Betty:   ┌He doesn't have┐ ↑any memory
172  |0:23:59:00|  Norman:  └(so            )┘
173  |0:24:00:00|  Betty:   problem right now.=
174  |0:24:01:00|  Norman:  =Yeah, which is very o┌:dd.
175  |0:24:02:00|  Betty:                         └Based on our mental
176                          ↑status exam,
177                          (0.3)
178  |0:24:04:00|  Coach:   °Hm mm°
179  |0:24:05:00|  Betty:   But yet his wife says that he's
180                          periodically gets goofy or >whatever it
181                          was that she said<
182                          (3.8)
183  |0:24:11:00|  Betty:   So,
184  |0:24:13:00|  Maria:   See a stroke can develop over a period of
185                          several ↓days usually progressing in a
186                          step like fashion=
187  |0:24:18:00|  Norman:  =(Unless it's  )
188  |0:24:19:00|  Maria:   With a deficit being added from time to
189                          time.
190                          (1.0)
191  |0:24:23:00|  Norman:  But then you would think the leg would be
192                          getting worse.
193                          (0.5)
194  |0:24:25:00|  Norman:  °I would think.°
195  |0:24:26:00|  Maria:   We:↓ll it could- I mean usually strokes
196                          are preceded by TIAs.
197                          (0.5)
198  |0:24:32:00|  Norman:  Yeah
199  |0:24:32:10|  Maria:   So then ┌it could've just been you know┐
200  |0:24:32:20|  Norman:          └Well  I  mean that's  a  yeah┘ =
201                          =that's a risk factor ↑for 'em. (0.7)
202  |0:24:35:20|  Norman:  The thing is that (1.0) we're seeing an-
203                          an acute leg deficit and now (.) we're
204                          seeing five over five strength.
205  |0:24:43:00|  Maria:   Hm-mm
206                          (1.5)
207  |0:24:43:20|  Norman:  ┌What ↑happened to it
208  |0:24:45:00|  Betty:   └obviously ┌there's no-
209  |0:24:45:00|  Maria:              └TI↑A
```

```
210  |0:24:47:00|   Betty:    Uh it's most likely there was no
211                           permanent dam⌐age from what=
212  |0:24:49:00|   Maria:             └Right.
213  |0:24:50:10|   Betty:    ⌐had happened.
214  |0:24:50:22|   Norman:   └But wh:y is his ↑speech now screwed up.
215                           (0.7)
216  |0:24:53:00|   Betty:    Is it screwed up
217  |0:24:54:00|   Norman:   It's screwed up ↑somehow
218  |0:24:55:00|   Betty:    °a little bit° ((hand gesture))
219  |0:24:56:00|   Norman:   =<like it wasn't ⌐before>
220  |0:24:57:00|   Maria:                   └He says it's gotten
221                           worse in the last couple of days=
222  |0:24:59:00|   Norman:   =Ye:ah.
223  |0:24:59:00|   Maria:    Some:thing's gotten worse I assume it's
224  |0:24:59:00|   Betty:    ⌐But yet when we-
225  |0:24:59:00|   Maria:    └↓his speech.
226  |0:25:02:00|   Betty:    But yet when we actually examine him I
227                           mean occasionally not even very often >he
228                           has trouble finding the right word and we
229                           do a mental status exam< (1.3) rarely
230                           >does he have trouble finding the right
231                           word and he can complete the ↑rest of the
232                           mental status exam with no problems<
233                           (1.0)
234  |0:25:17:00|   Betty:    So I don't kno:w.
235                           (7.0) ((Norman and Jenny looking at board))
236  |0:25:23:00|   Betty:    I think I would prob'ly lean more towards
237                           (1.0) trans- something transient that
238                           comes'n goes 'n we're catching him at a
239                           fairly good moment.
240                           (1.5)
241  |0:25:31:00|   Maria:    Uhh ⌐
242  |0:25:32:00|   Norman:       └Un⌐h::::::::::::: ┐ (("doubt" noise))
243  |0:25:32:00|   Betty:          └But I don't know.┘
244                           (5.0)
245  |0:25:38:00|   Betty:    An' it seems like to me that for (.) for:
246                           his wife to have been concerned about
247                           whatever was going on it has to be worse
248                           than it is right now. 'Cause it's just-
249                           (.) unless we just (.) don't have a very
```

```
250                          clear picture of what he's really like.
251                          Things just don't seem very ba:d.
252                          (1.0)
253  |0:25:51:00|   Maria:   Yeah see I don't t⌐hink we do have a clear-
254  |0:25:53:00|   Norman:               └I don't see it either.
255  |0:25:54:00|   Betty:   And I don't know how we can fix that.
256                          (5.0)
257  |0:26:01:00|   Betty:   Except if we asked every single question
258                          ⌐in the book.
259  |0:26:02:00|   Coach:   └Hmm ((smile))
260  |0:26:02:00|   Norman:  ((smile))
261  |0:26:03:00|   Betty:   (hu huh huh hh)
262  |0:26:04:00|   Coach:   Some patients are vague,
263  |0:26:06:00|   Betty:   Yep.
264                          (1.5)
265  |0:26:08:00|   Coach:   Just don't give you the answers you wanna
266                          hear.
```

DISCOURSE PROCESSES, 27(2), 119–133
Copyright © 1999, Lawrence Erlbaum Associates, Inc.

ANALYSES

Theory Presentation and Assessment in a Problem-Based Learning Group

Phillip J. Glenn
Department of Speech Communication
Southern Illinois University

Timothy Koschmann and Melinda Conlee
Department of Medical Education
School of Medicine
Southern Illinois University

In this study, we apply the procedures and assumptions of ethnomethodological conversation analysis to analyze a segment of interaction in a problem-based learning (PBL) meeting. In the segment, one member of the group presents a theory pertaining to the case under study. Before it is accepted or rejected, the same speaker presents a second theory to which other group members react with objections and disaffiliative laughter. The presenter consequently rejects the second theory and uses this rejection as a basis for returning to and implicitly accepting the first. Theory presentation and assessment are an integral part of the PBL group process of moving discursively from case history and symptoms to diagnosis and treatment. We observe that the presentation of a theory makes relevant a variety of sequential activities through which participants in instructional activities of this sort come to accept or discard the theory. Implications for teaching and tutorial practice are presented.

One of the stated objectives of problem-based learning (PBL) is for students to practice and develop skills for reasoning in clinical settings, including the ability to formulate a theory (in medical contexts, a diagnosis) that accounts for the

Correspondence and requests for reprints should be sent to Phillip J. Glenn, Department of Speech Communication, Southern Illinois University, Carbondale, IL 62901–6605. E-mail: pjglenn@siu.edu

evidence (medical history and symptoms; Barrows, 1994; Koschmann, Kelson, Feltovich, & Barrows, 1996). This reasoning largely occurs in and through meetings conducted by the group to discuss clinical cases. Thus, examination of interactions within these meetings should provide a basis for describing and assessing the reasoning students use.

REASONING IN PBL MEETINGS

PBL is undertaken in a variety of ways at different institutions (Barrows, 1986). In this article, we examine an example of interaction within a particular methodological approach to PBL that has been described in greater detail elsewhere (Barrows, 1994; Koschmann et al., 1996).

Within this particular implementation, the exploration of a case proceeds through several phases, namely problem formulating, self-directed learning, knowledge applying, abstracting, and reflecting (Koschmann et al., 1996). In the problem-formulating phase, the group begins by making inquiries into a case and developing a set of hypotheses about the source of the patient's problem. The case is then presented to the group in the form of a book designed to simulate the clinical interview and examination (Distlehorst & Barrows, 1982). During this phase, students may generate and, in some cases, defend theories about the patient's underlying disorder.

As the students develop a more complete picture of the case under study, they compile a list of areas in which they consider their knowledge to be deficient (Barrows, 1994; Koschmann, Glenn, & Conlee, in press). When this list grows long, the group recesses to allow the students time to independently research these issues, thereby entering into the phase of self-directed learning.

After this phase of independent work, the group members reconvene and attempt to apply their newly acquired knowledge to the case under study; that is, they begin the phase of knowledge applying. Armed with new knowledge, the students may be stimulated to ask new questions about the case. This, in turn, may inspire them to propose new theories or critique previously proposed theories.

The group may repeat cycles of problem formulating, self-directed learning, and knowledge applying several times before leaving a case. At appropriate junctures, the members of the group pause to reflect on their methods and contributions (i.e., reflecting phase) and to make attempts to abstract what they have learned from this particular case (abstracting phase). Discussion of student theories may also take place in these latter two phases, as when students evaluate their own theory-making contributions or when they attempt to articulate what they have learned from a particular case.

This iterative process of making inquiries into the patient's problem, proposing theories to account for this problem, and empirically testing these theories was designed to recapitulate the process used by skilled practitioners when problem solving in clinical practice (Barrows, 1990; Barrows & Feltovich, 1987). The faculty member's role in this process is to model this reasoning strategy while simultaneously helping the students to recognize areas of incomplete understanding of the case.[1]

In this article, we analyze a segment of interaction that took place during a phase of knowledge applying subsequent to a period of self-directed learning. Within this segment, one of the students advances two theories to account for the patient's problem. We describe how the theories are introduced and how the members of the group respond to these theories. Through this analysis, we hope to show some of the interactional sequences through which group members come to accept or reject theories.

APPLYING CONVERSATION ANALYSIS TO THE STUDY OF REASONING IN GROUPS

We treat reasoning as jointly constructed, grounded in and shaped by the sequential organization of interaction. Our approach reflects procedures and assumptions of ethnomethodological conversation analysis (CA; for discussions, see Atkinson & Heritage, 1984; Pomerantz & Fehr, 1997; Psathas, 1995). Briefly, CA methods emphasize close description of recordings of naturally occurring interactions with the aim of characterizing methods by which people organize their social worlds. CA researchers (a) create detailed transcripts noting speech, paralinguistic and visual behaviors, and aspects of timing and placement; (b) describe the ways people organize sequences of talk; and (c) generalizing from individual cases, derive inductive claims about recurrent features of social interaction. Analysis begins not with hypotheses but rather with open-ended description. The aim is to explicate how people produce interaction and what they accomplish in and through it. The emphasis is not on why things happen or people do what they do but on what they do and how they do it.

The analysis presented here arose from a research process involving the following steps. After viewing the videotaped group interaction, we selected the passage for analysis, drawn to it by Betty's proclamation of "my theory" and the subsequent discussion. We viewed and listened to the segment repeatedly while preparing the detailed transcript. During several intensive discussions among the authors (plus other researchers in informal listening sessions), we generated descriptions of ways participants organized the interaction. During this process, we relied on terms and descriptions from previous CA research that

---

[1]In medical education, the faculty member participating in a PBL group is referred to as the *tutor*. We have argued elsewhere (Koschmann et al., 1996) that this term may be somewhat misleading. In this article, therefore, we refer to the faculty member as the *learning coach* or simply the *coach*.

provide "tools" to aid analysis. Noticing participant orientation to theory presentation and treatment, we chose that as the focus for this article.

When presented in a PBL group meeting, a theory may provide a focus for
subsequent talk in which group members evaluate, modify, accept, or reject the
theory. These actions are produced by assessing the theory, displaying agreement
or disagreement, asking clarifying or critical questions, fitting evidence and reasoning to the theory, or producing alternative theories or accounts for data. In
the segment of interaction under consideration here, the participants consider a
theory presented by Betty, discuss the location of the hippocampus, entertain
another theory from Betty, attempt to distinguish a stroke from a TIA (transient
ischemic attack), and discuss the compatibility of symptoms with Betty's explanations. Interestingly, the group members return to the first theory only after
considering and rejecting the second. This suggests participant orientation to
treating the two theories as part of a larger structure. How they do so, and what
they might accomplish through such organization, are the focus of the remaining
discussion.

PRESENTATION OF EVIDENCE, REASONING, AND
THEORY: "MY THEORY"

Immediately prior to the start of this segment, the coach provides a *formulation*
(Heritage & Watson, 1978), or summary of preceding talk, followed by a conclusion:

```
Coach:   So he's got speech involvement 'n
         right leg involvement.
         (1.0)
Maria:   (Spee ch involvement)
Coach:        So-      So whatever his
         problem is: (.) we're pretty
         confident it's on the left side.
```

Formulations, by summarizing preceding talk, provide opportunity spaces for
interactants to move on to new, possibly related matters. Following the coach's
formulation, one of the students, Betty, introduces information from a book lying
in front of her:

```
1  |0:20:12:20|   Betty:  See, what it said in here
```

The imperative "see" brings the attention of the other group members to Betty;
"what it said in here" further places that focus on the book to which she refers.

Both can be heard as preliminary to presenting information from that book. Having thus displayed that she is about to present some information, Betty abandons that course to announce a "theory":

```
1  |0:20:12:20|   Betty:   See, what it said in here n-my theory
                           about this amnesic (.) dysnomic aphasia?
```

Because she has not yet presented her theory, this phrase can serve to project that the theory is to follow. Betty has prefaced two actions, each of which could warrant an extended turn at talk: presenting information from a book and offering a theory. She does take an extended turn to do both. She reads from the book, and she offers a theory:

```
1   |0:20:12:20|   Betty:   n-my theory
2                           ┌about this
3   |0:20:15:00|   (?):     └khu-(.hhhh)
4   |0:20:15:00|   Betty:   amnesic (.) dysnomic aphasia? (0.6) um it
5                           says the cause of lesion is usually deep
6                           in temporal lobe just like Maria was
7                           saying presumably interrupting
8                           connections of sensory speech areas with
9                           the hippocampal and parahippocampal
10                          regions. (1.0)
11                          and I think the hippocampus
12                          is like a lot more medial so if it was
13                          affecting that area it might be the
14                          anterior cerebral circulation.
```

She marks a return to reading (lines 4–5) by the phrase "it says." After reading, she stops (lines 6–7) to indicate that Maria (one of the other students), too, had suggested what this book apparently now confirms. This acknowledgment may serve to bring both Maria and "the book" into support for Betty's emerging theory. Betty quotes more from the book (lines 7–10), about the consequences of a lesion in the temporal lobe. She stops reading, and there is a 1-s pause (line 10). Under other circumstances, someone else might begin speaking at this moment. However, orienting to her announced-but-not-yet-presented theory, the others remain silent, granting her extended turn space. Betty now shows in at least two ways that she is no longer reading: She looks up to make eye contact with other group members, and by saying "I think," she marks what is to follow as her idea and as tentative (line 11). Her next statement concerns the location in the brain of the hippocampus, posited as a spatial comparison (line 12: "a lot more medial"). Thus, having presented evidence and reasoning, she offers as conclusion the theory (lines 12–14) that anterior cerebral circulation is the source of the problem for this patient.

Theory presentation is an integral part of theory construction. Betty's theory presentation occurs through an interweaving of two sequential activities: reading aloud and presenting a theory. She provides book evidence, notes that it supports something another group member had said, provides reasoning, and ends her extended turn with an explanation that stands as a theory. This roughly inductive pattern (evidence + reasoning → conclusion) places the actual theory at the end of the turn. The silence of other group members during her talk orients to this structure.

RESPONSE TO THEORY: IMPLICIT ENDORSEMENT AND INFORMATION SEARCH

As Betty nears completion of her turn, Norman says the word "anterior" in unison with her. This bit of overlapping speech occurs at what elsewhere has been described as a "recognition point" (Jefferson, 1973, pp. 58–59), an earliest possible moment at which a coparticipant may show understanding of the utterance in progress and may anticipate the substance of utterance completion.

```
12                 Betty:   so if it was
13                          affecting that area it might be the
14                          ┌anterior cerebral circulation.
15  |0:20:33:00|   Norman:  └Anterior.
```

Norman shows that he follows Betty's reasoning and that he, too, arrives—independently—at the same conclusion. This may also serve as a way to demonstrate alignment, if not outright agreement, with her theory.

The coach retrieves from Betty's preceding information knowledge that she had marked as tentative (see lines 13–14) and packages it in a question:

```
13                 Betty:   it might be the
14                          ┌anterior cerebral circulation.
15  |0:20:33:00|   Norman:  └Anterior.
16  |0:20:35:00|   Coach:   Where is the hippocampus.
```

This initiates an extended series of turns (not described here) devoted to identifying the hippocampus as depicted on flip charts of the brain. This activity is distinct from theory generation, though perhaps relevant to later theory evaluation. This segment terminates with Lill's pointing (with directions from Norman)

to one part of a picture and the coach confirming that the students have successfully located the hippocampus:

```
62  |0:21:33:00|  Norman:  Go to the crevice there.

63                         (1.0)

64  |0:21:34:00|  Norman:  That little loop?

65                         (1.0)

66  |0:21:36:00|  Norman:  Yeah.

67                         (1.0)

68  |0:21:37:00|  Coach:   That's it.
```

Although perhaps marking the end of the searching activity, the coach's confirming
"That's it" does not project a next action or select any particular other speaker as
next (for rules of speaker selection in conversation, see Sacks, Schegloff, &
Jefferson, 1974). Betty takes this opportunity to return to theory presentation.

ALTERNATIVE THEORY WITH REASONING AND EVIDENCE: "MY OTHER THEORY"

Betty now presents a second theory. As with the previous one, she marks ownership of the theory via a possessive pronoun. This theory stands in contrast to
her earlier one, offering "space occupying lesion" as an alternative explanation
to "vascular lesion."

```
69  |0:21:38:00|  Betty:  My other theory is that if it was- i- i-

70                        if it's not a vascular lesion but a space

71                        occupying lesion if it was (.) right

72                        there ((points to chart)) in the areas we

73                        were pointing to it would be like in a

74                        posterior limb of the interior capsule

75                        which would be where (.) the

76                        corticospinals to the leg would be going

77                        through that part.
```

Betty attempts to fit evidence to this new explanatory frame. Specifically, she
suggests localizing the problem in an area of the brain through which the nerve
pathways that control the leg travel. Leg clumsiness is one reported symptom for
this patient, and as such, it stands as a fact for which any theory may be held
accountable.

   If we entertain the possibility that presentation of a theory makes relevant its
subsequent acceptance, rejection, or modification, then we might see that Betty

presents this second theory while the first theory is possibly still "on the table." Thus, it may be that treatment of the second theory is in some direct way relevant to evaluating the first one. It may be, too, that this sequencing displays the two theories as part of some larger set of which both are members, and perhaps the only members. Betty links the two theories as a contrastive pair: She refers to this one as "my other theory" and she presents it as negation of her first theory, "not a vascular lesion but a space occupying lesion." In this instance, entertaining one theory involves invoking a domain, ruling out what is not, perhaps as a way to support an argument for what is.

RESPONSE TO THEORY: DISAFFILIATION, DISAGREEMENT, AND REJECTION

Although the first theory received implicit alignment from Norman and a follow-up question from the coach, this second theory receives two kinds of responses, each of which shows disaffiliation. First, Maria presents in a question a piece of evidence one would expect to find were this theory to be true:

```
75                 Betty:   where (.) the
76                          corticospinals to the leg would be going
77                          through that part.
78                          (1.0)
79  |0:21:53:00|   Maria:   Wouldn't you expect to see a lot=
82  |0:21:53:00|   Maria:   greater involvement if you got
85  |0:21:59:00|   Maria:   internal capsule?=
```

By this question, Maria raises an objection to Betty's second theory. Within a few syllables of the beginning of Maria's turn, Norman laughs:

```
75                 Betty:   where (.) the
76                          corticospinals to the leg would be going
77                          through that part.
78                          (1.0)
79  |0:21:53:00|   Maria:   Wouldn't you expect to ⌜see a lot=
80  |0:21:53:00|   Norman:                          ⌞(khh hh huh hh)
```

When laughter refers to talk, commonly that talk occurs in the immediately prior utterance (Schenkein, 1972, p. 365). Although we cannot see all the faces on the video, placement of the laugh—shortly following completion of Betty's turn and before Maria's turn in progress has displayed any recognizably laughable features—suggests that it may orient to Betty's talk. If so, it can be heard as disaffiliating from Betty's theory, treating it as not to be taken seriously. Consistent with this interpretation, the coach provides a stretched, exaggerated response (perhaps "whoa" or "o::kay"):

```
75                    Betty:  where (.) the
76                            corticospinals to the leg would be going
77                            through that part.
78                            (1.0)
79  |0:21:53:00|      Maria:  Wouldn't you expect to ⌈see a lot=
80  |0:21:53:00|      Norman:  ⌈                     ⌊(khh hh huh hh)
81  |0:21:53:00|      Coach:  ⌊Whoa ⌈kay
82  |0:21:53:00|      Maria:       ⌊greater involvement if you got
```

Thus, both Norman and the coach treat Betty's other theory as comical, whereas Maria treats it seriously but disputes it. Norman echoes her objection by the agreement token "yeah" (line 84). In short, Betty's second theory gets, not support, but disaffiliative laughter, objection, and silence.

Betty disattends the laughter and answers Maria's objection by producing an explanation for how a lesion could affect only a portion of the brain linking to the leg:

```
79  |0:21:53:00|      Maria:   Wouldn't you expect to see a lot=
82  |0:21:53:00|      Maria:   greater involvement if you got
84  |0:21:58:00|      Norman:  Yeah
85  |0:21:59:00|      Maria:   internal capsule?=
86  |0:22:02:00|      Betty:   =If it's small. >I mean if< it's
87                             in the very posterior li:mb, (.)
88                             posterior part of the posterior
89                             li:mb. (1.0) Because there's a-the-
90                             (2.0) somato:graphic whatever
91                             that word was, (.) arrangement of the
92                             corticospinals as they go
93  |0:22:13:00|      (?):    ⌈°right°
94  |0:22:13:00|      Betty:  ⌊through the (internal) capsule.
96  |0:22:16:00|      Betty:   If you get way to the posterior ↑part of
97                             the internal capsule the only thing
98                             that's there is motor and it's
100 |0:22:18:00|      Betty:   going to be the le:g.
```

Perhaps she does not win over the others to endorsing this theory, but at least they no longer treat it as comic. Norman aligns with Betty by repeating the word *motor* and assessing the information she has offered as "true."

```
 75                     Betty:  where (.) the
 76                             corticospinals to the leg would be going
 77                             through that part.
 78                             (1.0)
 79   |0:21:53:00|      Maria:  Wouldn't you expect to ⌜see a lot=
 80   |0:21:53:00|      Norman:                        ⌞(khh hh huh hh)
 81   |0:21:53:00|      Coach:  ⌞Whoa ⌜kay
 82   |0:21:53:00|      Maria:        ⌞greater in⌜volvement if you got
 83   |0:21:55:00|      Norman:                  ⌞(hh hh)
 84   |0:21:58:00|      Norman:  Yeah
 85   |0:21:59:00|      Maria:  internal capsule?<
 86   |0:22:02:00|      Betty:  =If it's small. >I mean if< it's
 87                             in the very posterior li:mb, (.)
 88                             posterior part of the posterior
 89                             li:mb. (1.0) Because there's a-the-
 90                             (2.0) somato:graphic whatever
 91                             that word was, (.) arrangement of the
 92                             corticospinals as they go
 93   |0:22:13:00|      (?):    ⌜°right°
 94   |0:22:13:00|      Betty:  ⌞through the (internal) ⌜capsule.
 95   |0:22:14:00|      Norman:                         ⌞Yeah
 96   |0:22:16:00|      Betty:  If you get way to the posterior ↑part of
 97                             the internal capsule the only thing
 98                             that's there ⌜is motor and it's
 99   |0:22:18:00|      Norman:             ⌞motor
100   |0:22:18:00|      Betty:  going t⌜o be the le:g.
101   |0:22:19:00|      Norman:        ⌞motor
102   |0:22:21:00|      Norman:  That's true
103                             (3.0)
```

After a pause, the coach raises another symptom issue for which Betty's second theory should account:

```
102   |0:22:21:00|      Norman:  That's true
103                             (3.0)
104   |0:22:24:00|      Coach:  So why do the leg findings go away?
```

Betty assesses this question as "good," then explicitly acknowledges that it undercuts the possibility of her second theory. She produces reasoning that goes against her own theory. Maria and Norman join with her in listing symptoms that ought to accompany a space-occupying lesion:

```
104  |0:22:24:00|   Coach:   So why do the leg findings go away?
105                          (1.0)
106  |0:22:27:00|   Betty:   That's a good question that kind of goes
107                          against it being some kind of a space
108                          occupying lesion because you would expect
109                          it to get progressive and then (you want
110                          it) to involve more areas.
111                          (0.4)
112  |0:22:34:00|   Betty:   So then it's ┌probably more likely
113  |0:22:35:00|   Maria:              └Headaches,=
114  |0:22:36:00|   Maria:   =you would expect
115  |0:22:36:15|   Norman:  You'd expect to have headaches
116  |0:22:37:00|   Betty:   °Maybe, yeah.°
117  |0:22:38:00|   Maria:   Seizures.
```

The second theory has failed to win support; even its author, Betty, has acknowledged its shortcomings.

(TENTATIVE) ACCEPTANCE OF FIRST THEORY:
"IF IT'S VASCULAR . . ."

After they list symptoms that "you would expect" (but, by implication, are not present), Betty concludes in favor of the first theory, which invoked circulation problems to account for the patient's symptoms:

```
113  |0:22:35:00|   Maria:   Headaches,=
114  |0:22:36:00|   Maria:   =you would expect
115  |0:22:36:15|   Norman:  You'd expect to have headaches
116  |0:22:37:00|   Betty:   °Maybe, yeah.°
117  |0:22:38:00|   Maria:   Seizures.
118                          (0.7)
119  |0:22:41:00|   Betty:   Um (0.8) it's more likely to be vascular.
```

The coach legitimizes this conclusion by his subsequent actions. The token "okay" routinely displays readiness to move on from current to next items of topic or business (see Beach, 1993); the coach uses it here, and he asks a question that presumes "vascular" to be at least plausible enough to provide a basis for further theory construction:

```
119  |0:22:41:00|   Betty:   Um (0.8) it's more likely to be vascular.
120                          (2.5)
```

```
121  |0:22:45:00|    Coach:   °Oka⌐y°
122  |0:22:46:00|    Maria:     └°With his history an⌐d social°
123  |0:22:46:15|    Coach:                        └So
124  |0:22:48:00|    Coach:   So if it's vascular did he have a ↑stroke
125                            or is he having a TIA. What is the
126                            difference between those two things
127                            anyway.
```

The participants have entertained two theories, rejecting the second and, although not explicitly endorsing the first, at least accepting it enough to use it as a basis for further questioning and theory construction. As our analysis concludes, the group continues discussing the case from the framework of Betty's theory that this patient's problem involves a vascular lesion.

DISCUSSION

PBL participants in this episode orient to theorizing as a central activity. One student presents a theory and supports it with evidence and reasoning, another student displays concurrence with her reasoning, and the coach initiates discussion devoted to clarifying information relevant to the theory. On completion of this clarifying task, the same student presents a second theory posed as an alternative to the first. This second theory gets no support from other participants, who respond with silence, critical questioning, and disaffiliative laughter. The presenter herself discounts the second theory and concludes that the first one is valid. The coach then uses the first theory, implicitly "accepted" for the moment, as a basis for a subsequent question, which leads to presentation of additional information.

In this excerpt, Betty presents her two theories as products of her individual reasoning ("My theory" ... "My other theory"). However, the "processing" of the theories (including such actions as agreeing, disagreeing, questioning, modifying, etc.) is thoroughly interactional. This collaborative learning exemplifies one primary virtue of the PBL process: Theories survive or fall in a rhetorical, intersubjective, communicative context. This analysis shows Betty's first theory as succeeding not because of any inherent "truth" or rightness it possesses but as a result of talk that follows it and the second theory.

The group members orient to theory presentation not only by what they do but also by what they do not do. When Betty announces a forthcoming theory ("My theory"), the others grant her extended turn space to present the theory; when theory presentation is complete, they treat each theory as a topic for subsequent discussion. Were group members to interrupt her before she could present either theory or ignore the theories once presented, such moves might provide evidence that participants orient to something other than theorizing as central at these moments in the interaction. To sum up, their displayed orientation to theorizing in this episode is not inevitable but is a product of group members' methodical practices.

The presentation and treatment of theories seems to be one overarching sequential activity in this interaction, but it is not the only one. Glossed over rather quickly in this article are sequences devoted to presenting information (one student reports on distinctions between strokes and TIAs) and clarifying uncertainties (such as the group work of pointing out the hippocampus on flip charts of the brain).[2] In other parts of the PBL meeting, there also are instances of casual talk, play and laughter, and metalevel reflection on the process. Related to the preceding point, it can be argued that this interaction involves at least two organizing frameworks or sequential contexts: One is group problem solving or decision making; the other is instructional, teacher–student interaction. The two frameworks may differ such that orienting to both creates interactional problems for participants. How they make one or the other framework relevant at particular moments provides an interesting question for further exploration.

In this excerpt, both theory presentations and turns at talk are differentially distributed. One student presents two theories; no one else does. Two students do almost all of the responding to these theories. Were these trends to continue for this group, we might easily identify Betty, Maria, and Norman as the most active members. Such distributions provide ways to create, maintain, and modify social interactional roles such as leader, follower, critic, and so on, within a group setting. Such a division of labor might be described as a form of "distributed cognition" (Salomon, 1993) in that multiple parties participate in the development of a final theory. Successfully solving problems as a group is thought to contribute to the development of skills that will eventually enable the members of the group to enjoy similar success in individual problem solving (Feltovich, Spiro, Coulson, & Feltovich, 1996). However, this claim assumes participation by all group members. In the excerpt analyzed here, three members contribute only minimally. Were this to continue, the learning coach might intervene to ensure more equitable participation by all the members of the group.

Although it is not our focus here, one can readily appreciate and study the work involved in serving as a coach for a PBL group. The coach intervenes at particular moments and guides the group work in particular ways. According to the rules of PBL, the coach cannot provide answers for the students but can display at key points essential reasoning processes (Barrows, 1994; Koschmann et al., in press). In this excerpt, he does so at several points through his summaries and questions.

---

[2]The work undertaken by the group to determine the location of the hippocampus might serve as an example of what we have described elsewhere (Koschmann et al., in press) as a "knowledge display segment."

We ground our claims in a descriptive, inductive method. Such an approach holds great potential for helping researchers understand the interactive processes in PBL group work that are so crucial to its success. We hope that this article serves both to illustrate the possibilities of close description of PBL interaction and to demonstrate conversation analytic description and reasoning. By analyzing additional instances of theory presentation and treatment in PBL groups, we may begin to explore the extent to which the features described earlier are routine parts of such interactions. Presenting one's own ideas and responding to others' ideas through questions and assessments are activities common in ordinary conversation as well as in specialized interactions such as PBL groups. Thus, what we learn from analyzing these sessions helps us understand not only PBL groups but talk in interaction in a variety of contexts.

ACKNOWLEDGMENTS

Support for this work was in the form of a Spencer National Academy of Education Post-Doctoral Fellowship to Timothy Koschmann and in equipment funding from the Abbott Foundation. An abbreviated version of this analysis was presented at Computer Support for Collaborative Learning '95, Bloomington, Indiana, October 1995. We thank Howard Barrows, Carl Frederiksen, and Annemarie Palincsar for reading an earlier draft of this article and for providing helpful suggestions.

REFERENCES

Atkinson, J. M., & Heritage, J. (1984). *Structures of social action: Studies in conversation analysis.* Cambridge, England: Cambridge University Press.

Barrows, H. S. (1986). A taxonomy of problem-based learning methods. *Medical Education, 20,* 481–486.

Barrows, H. S. (1990). Inquiry: The pedagogical importance of a skill central to clinical practice. *Medical Education, 24,* 3–5.

Barrows, H. S. (1994). *Practice-based learning: Problem-based learning applied to medical education.* Springfield: Southern Illinois University School of Medicine.

Barrows, H. S., & Feltovich, P. J. (1987). The clinical reasoning process. *Medical Education, 21,* 86–91.

Beach, W. A. (1993). Transitional regularities for 'casual' 'Okay' usages. *Journal of Pragmatics, 19,* 325–252.

Distlehorst, L. H., & Barrows, H. S. (1982). A new tool for problem-based self-directed learning. *Journal of Medical Education, 57,* 466–488.

Feltovich, P., Spiro, R., Coulson, R., & Feltovich, J. (1996). Collaboration within and among minds: Mastering complexity, individually and in groups. In T. Koschmann (Ed.), *CSCL: Theory and practice of an emerging paradigm* (pp. 25–44). Mahwah, NJ: Lawrence Erlbaum Associates, Inc.

Heritage, J. C., & Watson, D. R. (1978). Formulations as conversational objects. In G. Psathas (Ed.), *Everyday language: Studies in ethnomethodology* (pp. 123–162). New York: Irvington.

Jefferson, G. (1973). A case of precision timing in ordinary conversation: Overlapped tag-positioned address terms in closing sequences. *Semiotica, 9,* 47–96.

Koschmann, T., Glenn, P., & Conlee, M. (in press). When is a problem-based tutorial not tutorial? Analyzing the tutor's role in the emergence of a learning issue. In C. Hmelo & D. Evensen (Eds.), *Problem-based learning: Gaining insights on learning interactions through multiple methods of inquiry.* Mahwah, NJ: Lawrence Erlbaum Associates, Inc.

Koschmann, T., Kelson, A. C., Feltovich, P. J., & Barrows, H. S. (1996). Computer-supported problem-based learning: A principled approach to the use of computers in collaborative learning. In T. D. Koschmann (Ed.), *CSCL: Theory and practice of an emerging paradigm* (pp. 83–124). Mahwah, NJ: Lawrence Erlbaum Associates, Inc.

Pomerantz, A., & Fehr, B. J. (1997). Conversation analysis: An approach to the study of social action as sense making practices. In T. A. van Dijk (Ed.), *Discourse as social interaction* (pp. 64–91). Thousand Oaks, CA: Sage.

Psathas, G. (1995). *Conversation analysis: The study of talk-in-interaction.* Thousand Oaks, CA: Sage.

Sacks, H., Schegloff, E. A., & Jefferson, G. (1974). A simplest systematics for organization of turn-taking for conversation. *Language, 50,* 696–735.

Salomon, G. (Ed.). (1993). *Distributed cognitions: Psychological and educational considerations.* Cambridge, England: Cambridge University Press.

Schenkein, J. N. (1972). Towards an analysis of natural conversation and the sense of *heheh. Semiotica, 6,* 344–377.

DISCOURSE PROCESSES, 27(2), 135–160

Learning to Reason Through Discourse in a Problem-Based Learning Group

Carl H. Frederiksen

Applied Cognitive Science Research Group
Department of Educational and Counselling Psychology
McGill University
Montreal, Canada

Techniques of propositional analysis, analysis of conceptual structure and infer-ences, and frame analysis were applied to the discourse of a problem-based learning group in medicine. The results provide evidence of (a) the coach's use of a *differ-ential diagnosis frame* to organize the group's diagnostic inquiry procedures, (b) the coconstruction of explanatory *case models* linking causes to clinical symptoms through interactive discussion of the case, (c) processes of collaborative reasoning in evaluating alternative causal hypotheses for clinical evidence, and (d) a partici-pation structure in which speakers made different contributions to the collaborative problem solving through their contributions to the conversation. The results show how the content of task-oriented dialogue can be analyzed to reveal how participants in an interactive discussion of a clinical case use diagnostic inquiry procedures to coconstruct models of a case and reason to evaluate alternative causal hypotheses. The analysis provides insights about how this discourse supports students' devel-opment of biomedical knowledge and diagnostic expertise.

Problem-based learning (PBL) groups are complex social situations of profes-sional education that are organized to simulate types of collaborative problem solving that occur as a part of the everyday practice of members of a professional community. Experience in such groups is intended to facilitate students' transi-tions to appropriate roles within a professional community and to provide them with a rich context in which to develop robust professional knowledge and ex-pertise in using it to reason and solve problems (Collins, Brown, & Newman, 1989). A central assumption of PBL is that, for students to develop expertise in a professional domain, they must not only acquire a rich body of conceptual and

Correspondence and requests for reprints should be sent to Carl H. Frederiksen, Applied Cognitive Science Research Group, Department of Educational and Counselling Psychology, McGill University, 3700 McTavish Street, Montreal, Quebec, Canada H3A 1Y2. E-mail: ed76@musica.mcgill.ca

procedural knowledge and facility in applying it to analyze and solve authentic problems but they must also become proficient in functioning within the kinds of social contexts in which groups of professionals typically collaborate to solve problems. An excellent example of a PBL situation is the use of PBL groups to develop clinical expertise in medicine (Barrows, 1985, 1986; Barrows & Tamblyn, 1980; Koschmann, Myers, Feltovich, & Barrows, 1993–1994). Medical students participating in these groups work cooperatively to solve clinical problems. With guidance and assistance from a coach (who is also a member of the group), students are presented with realistic examples of diagnostic problems and have access to clinical case information, textual sources, results of laboratory tests, and other information that they use to arrive at a diagnosis. In this context, students discuss relevant biomedical and clinical knowledge to reason about a case (Barrows & Feltovich, 1987). This shared diagnostic reasoning occurs through interactive discourse among the participants in the group.

Any PBL situation consists of a complex context in which a group's learning and collaborative problem solving take place. This context includes (a) a physical environment (e.g., a physical and spatial setting of individuals, objects, and events), (b) representational resources (e.g., a chart recording case information, a scan of the brain, and a medical text used for reference), (c) a task-action environment (e.g., a diagnostic problem to be solved and sequences of actions taken to solve the problem), (d) the prior knowledge of members of the group (e.g., their biomedical and clinical knowledge pertaining to a case and their knowledge of procedures for developing a differential diagnosis), and (e) a social and interactional environment (e.g., the social organization of the group, the status and roles of its members, the social and institutional setting of the group, and patterns of social interaction within the group). Within any such context, the members of a PBL group collaborate as they try to understand clinical cases and solve diagnostic problems, communicating with one another by means of *interactive task-oriented dialogue*. This socially constructed discourse is the principal medium within the PBL situation by which the members of the group can communicate conceptual and procedural knowledge relevant to a problem or case under consideration and by which they can learn to apply their knowledge (e.g., to understand a clinical case, reason appropriately, and solve diagnostic problems). Furthermore, together with any written texts, charts, or other representational resources that are either produced by or made available to the members of the group, this discourse provides the students with a source of biomedical and clinical knowledge that is situated within practical contexts in which it is used to build conceptual models of clinical cases, to reason, and to solve diagnostic problems (Brown, Collins, & Duguid, 1989).

Like other forms of discourse, this socially constructed PBL dialogue defines both a *local discourse context* and a *discourse macrostructure* for the participants in the group (Frederiksen, 1986; van Dijk & Kintsch, 1983). As a discourse evolves over the course of interaction within a PBL session, both of these function to constrain and organize interaction among the participants at any point in the dialogue as they collaborate in attempting to understand and solve a problem. First, the participants' contributions to this dialogue must be "locally coherent" in the sense that they are appropriate to their local discourse contexts. For example, the members of a PBL group must express propositional meanings that are pertinent to the topic currently being discussed, related inferentially to what was said previously, and appropriate to the current conversational context. Second, their contributions to the dialogue must be "globally coherent" in the sense that they are pertinent within the framework of the discourse macrostructure. For example, in clinical problem-solving situations in medicine, the discourse macrostructure reflects the structure of the participants' biomedical and clinical knowledge relevant to modeling a particular clinical case, the structure of their reasoning to arrive at a diagnosis of the case, and the structure of the diagnostic procedures they use to guide problem-solving actions. Contributing to the construction of this discourse macrostructure, therefore, involves contributing to the group's construction of alternative models of a clinical case, to the group's ongoing processes of clinical reasoning, and to their application of a coherent method for clinical problem solving. If any members of the group (such as the coach or more experienced students) already possess "expert" domain knowledge, their contributions to the task-oriented dialogue will reflect that knowledge and thus help ensure that the discourse macrostructure embodies models of knowledge structures, problem-solving methods, and reasoning processes that are similar to those of experienced professionals in the field. In this way, a PBL discourse can provide both a local and a global framework within which students can expand and refine their biomedical and clinical knowledge, learn to reason appropriately, analyze and solve diagnostic problems, and communicate knowledge appropriately within a professional group. In addition, through their participation in this discourse, group members can learn to contribute effectively to the collaborative reasoning and problem-solving activities of the group.

To accomplish this complex sociocognitive act, individual participants in a PBL group must be able to comprehend this evolving, socially constructed discourse as it reflects the knowledge, reasoning, and problem-solving activity of the group. That is, at any point in time, participants must be able to understand the reasoning process as it is unfolding through the discourse interaction of the participants, both in terms of local reasoning operations and in terms of how this local reasoning contributes to carrying out the procedures for diagnostic inquiry that are being applied to solve the problem (reflected in the discourse macrostructure). In addition, through their discourse productions, the participants must be able to provide information that is contextually appropriate to contribute to the group's interactive processes of collaborative reasoning and problem solving. A PBL discourse consists of a dynamic sequence of conversational exchanges that evolves over time as the participants in the group collaborate to develop alternative models of a case and use them in solving a diagnostic problem.

Furthermore, these exchanges may be extended over more than one session of the group. The manner and extent to which the PBL discourse provides a structure to support (i.e., "scaffold") the participants' contributions to the group's problem solving may undergo important changes over the course of a single session or a series of sessions. For example, a PBL group often includes a coach; as the members of a group acquire greater knowledge and experience, the coach's type and degree of assistance to the group may change (e.g., by shifting from a coaching to a mediator role). Furthermore, as participants in a PBL group become more experienced, they may increasingly use their contributions to the discourse as a means of communicating their prior knowledge and independent reasoning to other members of the group.

Over the course of participation in a series of PBL sessions, students acquire declarative and procedural knowledge in a domain (or a collection of subdomains) and develop skill in applying this knowledge to solve clinical problems, both individually and collaboratively. The problem-solving skill that is acquired includes both skill in contributing to the collaborative reasoning and problem-solving activity of the group and skill in independently solving new or novel problems without the support and constraints of participation in the group. Over a course of many sessions, a PBL group may gradually display collective dialogue and problem-solving behavior that is similar to that which occurs in groups of experienced professionals. In addition, individual members may learn to contribute to the group in ways that are typical of the contributions of experienced professionals. Furthermore, each member may become skilled in understanding and solving clinical problems independently in a manner comparable to experienced professionals. If all of these conditions were met, we could say that experience in a PBL group had met its objectives of developing both cognitive and socio-cognitive expertise.

Given the central importance of interactive discourse in PBL groups, many questions will need to be answered if we are to adequately understand and predict the nature of discourse, cognition, and learning in these complex PBL situations. For example, how does a PBL discourse support students' individual and collaborative construction of biomedical and clinical knowledge, and what cognitive processes are needed to make effective use of this support? How does participation in this discourse enable students to develop expertise in applying clinical and biomedical knowledge and learn to reason appropriately to solve diagnostic problems? How does experience in such PBL groups lead to the development of skill in contributing as a member of a professional group to situations of collaborative clinical reasoning and problem solving?

This article examines these questions from a cognitive perspective by analyzing the content of interactive discourse within a PBL situation and relating it to the structure of the discourse interaction. First, to investigate students' construction of knowledge, we analyzed the propositional content of the PBL discourse to examine what clinical and biomedical information the students encountered and what propositional information each student and the coach added to the discussion of the case. Then, we examined how these propositions contributed to the construction of an integrated conceptual structure (i.e., a semantic or propositional network) to develop alternative explanatory models of the clinical case. Second, to investigate how the discourse provided students with models of clinical reasoning and problem solving, we examined how and to what extent students' propositions, inferences, and problem-solving actions reflected the use of a coherent procedure frame to guide their process of diagnostic inquiry and clinical problem solving. We also analyzed the structure and direction of students' inferences relating successive propositions as they reasoned to construct alternative diagnostic hypotheses and to evaluate them against the clinical evidence. Finally, to investigate how the students were able to contribute to the collaborative problem solving of this simulated professional group, we related the content of the group's dialogue and reasoning to the structure of the conversation, to the group's patterns of social interaction, and to the different roles and contributions made by each member of the group. In this way, we attempt to show how the coach and individual students in a PBL group contributed to a collaborative process of clinical reasoning and problem solving through their contributions to this dialogue. Taken together, these analyses contribute to understanding how the structure and content of PBL discourse support and constrain students' learning processes, thus contributing to a generalizable cognitive theory of PBL.

ANALYSIS OF THE "MY THEORY" VIDEOTAPE

The PBL videotape "My Theory" provides one example of a PBL situation in medicine. In focusing on this videotape, we are concerned with the cognitive representations and processes that are required for a student to participate effectively in the PBL discourse of one group that is attempting to solve a diagnostic reasoning problem in this one particular domain of medicine (neurology). An extension of this analysis to a study of the cognitive processes involved in learning in this domain (i.e., constructing domain knowledge and developing skill in solving problems of clinical diagnosis in this domain) would have to consider not only the learning that takes place within a single PBL session (or the sequence of sessions devoted to a single problem) but also the development of general diagnostic expertise over a course of several PBL problems. We limit the scope of this analysis to a single session.

   The methods applied to analyze this discourse are similar to those used to study the structure, comprehension, and production of written texts, specifically propositional analysis, analysis of conceptual structure and inferences, and frame analysis (in this case the structure of the procedure frame used to guide the solution of the diagnostic problem; Frederiksen & Breuleux, 1990; Frederiksen & Donin, 1991). The theoretical approach comes from discourse processing theory and research on problem solving. By relating the propositional and conceptual content, as well as the inferences and frame structure of the PBL discourse to the interactive structure of the dialogue, we may examine the clinical reasoning process as it evolves through the discourse interaction of the participants. In this way, the clinical reasoning may be examined both in terms of local chains of reasoning (based on the propositional microstructure) and in terms of how this local reasoning contributes to carrying out a general diagnostic inquiry procedure (i.e., the macrostructure) that is being used to build and evaluate alternative models of the case. Furthermore, we may examine how different individuals contributed to this process of collaborative reasoning and the problem-solving activity of the group through their participation in the dialogue. This analysis considers: (a) the group's use of a *differential diagnosis frame* to organize their reasoning and problem-solving processes, (b) the group's construction of conceptual structures (i.e., *mental models*) to explain the clinical case information, (c) the PBL discourse as a medium for collaborative reasoning, and (d) how each participant contributed through the dialogue to the group's collaborative problem solving, construction of clinical case models, and clinical reasoning processes.

Use of the Differential Diagnosis Frame

To investigate the structure of the clinical problem-solving procedure used by the group, an analysis in terms of a hierarchical procedure frame (similar to a planning net) was undertaken. In research on discourse comprehension and problem solving, a procedure frame model is often developed based on an analysis of the structure of goals and actions required to perform problem-solving tasks in a domain and on analyses of problem-solving protocols of experts (i.e., experienced problem solvers) and students performing specific problem-solving tasks from the domain. The model used in this analysis was based on an analysis of the structure of the problem-solving actions reflected in the videotape and informed by previous analyses of diagnostic reasoning. Once a procedure frame model has been developed, discourse segments and problem-solving actions of the group are matched to procedures in the model, resulting in a *trace analysis* of the sequence of procedures and actions that were carried out in solving the problem. Thus, a procedure frame analysis provides information about how and to what extent the actions of the participants reflected the application of a coherent procedure for diagnostic inquiry. It also reveals how and to what extent the discourse structure reflects this procedure frame (i.e., the extent to which its macrostructure was based on the procedure frame).

    A procedure frame represents a model of the decomposition of the actions (procedures or goals) needed to complete a problem-solving task (Frederiksen & Breuleux, 1990). This decomposition is represented as a tree structure in which nodes represent procedures (potential actions) and branches represent decomposition into subprocedures. For the differential diagnosis task (see Figure 1), the

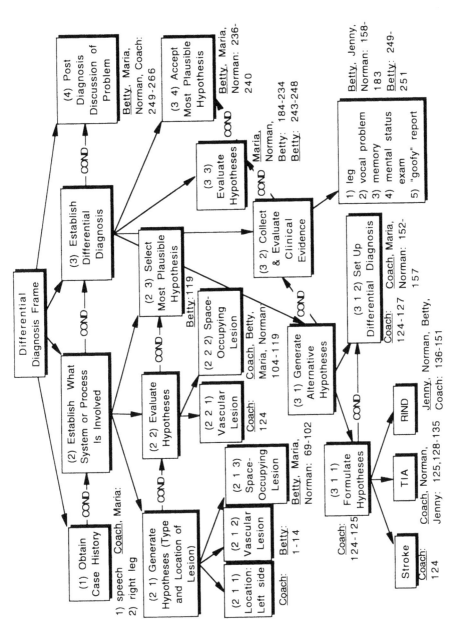

FIGURE 1 The problem-based learning group's use of a differential diagnosis frame.

141

top-level procedure is used to establish a differential diagnosis for the case (the goal) given the presenting clinical information of a case (the initial problem state). This top-level procedure decomposes into four main component subprocedures:

1. Review the patient's medical history;
2. Establish what system or process is involved;
3. Establish a diagnosis; and
4. Conduct a postdiagnosis discussion of the case.

The second of these (i.e., establish what system or process is involved) decomposes into three components:

2.1 Generate hypotheses (concerning the type and location of the lesion);
2.2 Evaluate these hypotheses in relation to the presenting evidence; and
2.3 Select the most plausible hypothesis.

The third main subprocedure (i.e., establish a diagnosis) decomposes into four components:

3.1 Generate diagnostic hypotheses;
3.2 Collect clinical evidence relevant to the hypotheses;
3.3 Evaluate the hypotheses; and
3.4 Select the most plausible hypothesis.

The procedure frame model also includes conditional dependencies among the nodes branching from a common parent.

The results of a procedure frame analysis of the "My Theory" dialogue are given in Figure 1. For each node, the line numbers bracketing conversational sequences matched to each node are given together with the names of the participants in the sequence. These sequences consisted of stretches of thematically related talk that accomplished the subtask corresponding to the procedure node. The initiator of each sequence is given first and is underlined. By following the order of line numbers, the sequence (i.e., trace) in which the nodes in the frame were applied in working on this diagnostic problem can be seen. As may be seen in Figure 1, this dialogue consisted mostly of talk associated with the actions required to carry out this procedure for differential diagnosis. The trace analysis shows that the procedure was applied in a left-to-right, depth-first fashion and that the dialogue reflected a relatively complete application of the procedure for differential diagnosis (as represented by the procedure frame model). Thus, the problem solving consisted of an orderly sequence of actions that corresponded to the hierarchical organization of the procedure and its ordering of subprocedures (in terms of conditional dependencies). How was it that this group was able to apply such a consistent approach to differential diagnosis? As discussed later, the coach appears to have guided the application of this procedure by initiating the conversational sequences that introduced shifts to new procedures in the sequence depicted by the trace analysis. Finally, not all of the dialogue could be matched to the differential diagnosis frame: There was an extended series of conversational exchanges (lines 16–68 in the protocol) that consisted of a coach-initiated discussion that involved finding the location of the hippocampus on a chart containing scans of a brain. This discussion was linked to Betty's first hypothesis concerning the type and location of the lesion (see the next section). Although this discussion did not directly contribute to solving the diagnostic problem, it enabled students to refine their knowledge of the anatomy of this region of the brain. We may speculate that the coach introduced this discussion of anatomy for pedagogical reasons; he was embedding an anatomy lesson within the larger task of solving the diagnostic problem.

Construction of Explanatory Models of the Case

The clinical reasoning task requires the construction and evaluation of alternative conceptual models of a case and diagnostic hypotheses based on these *case models* using relevant biomedical and clinical knowledge. The frame analysis of the discourse enabled us to identify the particular procedures that were carried out by the group through their dialogue. Although the differential diagnosis frame provided a procedural macrostructure that organized the talk and problem-solving activity, to see how case models were collaboratively constructed and evaluated by the members of the group requires an analysis of the propositional content of the utterances that were contributed by each member to the group's discussion of alternative models of the case. These propositions represent the encoded meanings directly expressed by the contributors to the discussion. As such, they reflect the articulation by the individuals concerned of their contributions to a public discussion of alternative conceptual models of the case. Of course, these public expressions do not fully represent the reasoning processes of each individual involved; they reflect each individual's contributions to models being collaboratively constructed by the group through their discussion. Therefore, we may examine the propositional content of these discussions as reflections of collaborative processes for constructing alternative explanatory models of the case. With these considerations in mind, we analyzed how the participants in these discussions contributed to the construction of alternative explanatory models of the case through their propositions (Frederiksen & Donin, 1991; Frederiksen & Emond, 1993; Kintsch, 1991).

There were three stretches of talk that were primarily concerned with the construction of conceptual models of the case: (a) *Betty's first theory* (lines 1–14), in which Betty presented a textbook account of one model (a vascular model) that she judged was pertinent to the case and then proceeded to modify it; (b)

Betty's other theory (lines 69–119), in which Betty presented an alternative theory (a space-occupying lesion), elaborated it in response to reactions of other members of the group (Maria and Norman), evaluated it in response to a question raised by the coach, and then dropped it; and (c) *Betty's and Norman's elaboration of diagnostic hypotheses* in response to a coach-initiated discussion of possible alternative diagnoses of the case under the assumption that the lesion was vascular (lines 123–151). By locating these line numbers in Figure 1, it can be seen where these discussions occurred in relation to the overall inquiry procedure that was being applied by the group as they developed a differential diagnosis for the case. Note that the presenting evidence in this case included "speech involvement" and "right leg involvement" (the coach, lines preceding "My Theory" segment). In these discussions of alternative case models, the overall structure of a case model contained some or all of the following causally related components (--CAU→ denotes a cause–effect relation):

Causal Event --CAU→	Lesion	--CAU→ Brain Effects	--CAU→ Clinical Symptoms
(vascular,	(area of brain	(e.g., cortico-	(behavioral effects)
tumor)	affected)	spinal path-	
		ways are	
		affected)	

Causal events (e.g., a stroke) were often linked directly to effects on the brain (e.g., a lesion affecting the hippocampal region) or to clinical symptoms (e.g., showing neurological effects that become better in 24 hr). Summaries of analyses of these discourse segments are presented in the form of conceptual graph representations of the conceptual models of the case that the participants in these discourse segments constructed through their dialogue (Sowa, 1983). The analyses involved first a propositional analysis of the talk, and second, the construction of a conceptual graph to link these propositions into a network.

The analysis of the first segment, Betty's first theory, is presented in Figure 2. The ellipses represent concepts and the links between them represent semantic relations present in the propositions. Boxes are used to represent nodes in the conceptual graph that are entire propositions. Quoted nodes and quoted links (e.g., "CAU") represent concepts and relations that were read by Betty from a medical textbook; all other unquoted nodes and links were added by Betty as she modified the textbook theory. The textbook model began with a labeling of the clinical symptoms ("amnesiac dysnomic aphasia"); it then referred to the cause of the lesion in terms of its location ("usually deep in the temporal lobe"), the lesion itself, and finally, its effects on the brain ("presumably interrupting connections of sensory speech areas with the hippocampal and parahippocampal regions"). Betty proceeded to modify the theory, reasoning that the brain area affected by the lesion was more specific, and therefore, the cause might have been the anterior cerebral circulation: "I think the hippocampus is like a lot more medial so if it was affecting that area it might be the anterior cerebral circulation"

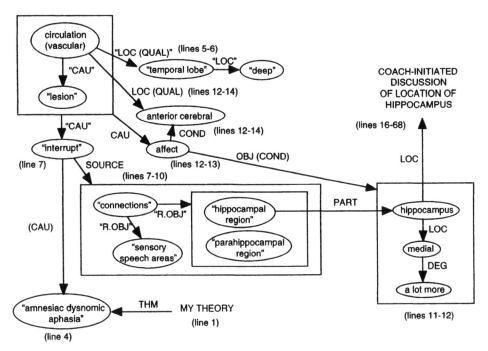

FIGURE 2   Betty's modification of a textbook theory: amnesiac dysnomic aphasia.

(lines 11–14). This conditional inference is represented by the qualified locative relation LOC (QUAL) corresponding to lines 12–14 in the graph. This is an example of how one individual presented and then modified a textbook model in applying it to this case.

The second segment, Betty's other theory (see Figure 3), provides an example of how a case model was constructed collaboratively by a subgroup consisting of Betty, Maria, and Norman, with an intervention by the coach. In this figure, Betty's contributions to the conceptual model are in normal text; contributions of others are represented in italics. This discourse consisted of four sections. In the first section (lines 69–77), Betty presented her alternative theory that the lesion was "not a vascular lesion but a space occupying lesion" (lines 69–71). She argued that, if this lesion were located "in a posterior limb of the internal capsule," this would have a particular effect on the brain because it would be where "the corticospinals to the leg would be going through that part" (lines 73–77). The second section (lines 79–103) was initiated by Maria, who gave her reaction (Reaction 1, Figure 3) to Betty's theory by stating that other symptomatic effects would be expected to occur ("Wouldn't you expect to see a lot greater involvement if you got internal capsule?" lines 79–85). This was followed by Betty's first response (Response 1) in which she elaborated her model of the size and location of the space-occupying lesion ("If it's small. >I mean if< it's in the

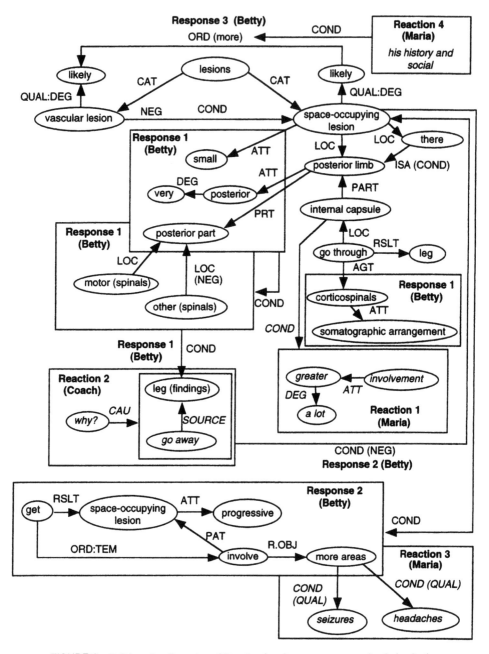

FIGURE 3 Collaborative discussion of Betty's other theory: space-occupying lesion in the posterior limb of the internal capsule.

very posterior li:mb, (.) posterior part of the posterior li:mb," lines 86–89) and its effects on the corticospinals ("Because there's a-the- somato:graphic whatever that word was, (.) arrangement of the corticospinals as they go °right° through the (internal) capsule," lines 89–94). Here the transcript is unclear who said "°right°." Either it was uttered by Betty or by someone else as an expression of agreement with Betty's thought. In her response, she also stated that only motor pathways would be affected, thus answering Maria's objection ("If you get way to the posterior ↑part of the internal capsule the only thing that's there is motor and it's going to be the le:g," lines 96–100). The third section was initiated by the coach's question concerning possibly contradictory clinical effects (Reaction 2): "So why do the leg findings go away?" (line 104). Betty's response to the coach's question (Response 2) acknowledged that this finding is inconsistent with a space-occupying lesion (the negative conditional COND NEG in Figure 3) and that you would expect other effects if it were a space-occupying lesion: "You would expect it to get progressive and then . . . to involve more areas" (lines 108–110). Maria then added two additional clinical symptoms that are conditional on a lesion in the internal capsule in Reaction 3: "Headaches, you would expect seizures" (lines 113, 114, 117). This was followed by Betty's rejection of her second case model in Response 3: "It's more likely to be vascular" (line 119). Maria adds in Reaction 4: "°With his history and social° . . ." (line 122). Norman's contributions to this discussion consisted mostly of repetitions and agreement responses, serving to establish his status as a participant in this particular discussion but not adding any new information to the discussion.

Betty constructed her initial model of the case by elaborating a textbook model prior to the session. She began by presenting her initial model to the group (i.e., the vascular lesion). Then she presented her second model (i.e., the space-occupying lesion) and elaborated it in response to Maria's reactions. Maria also contributed directly to elaborating the second model. Finally, the coach posed a question by asking for an explanation of some contradictory clinical evidence, which led Betty and Maria to further elaborate the second model and, subsequently, to Betty's evaluation and subsequent rejection of this model. Thus, the interaction provided a conversational framework for modifications of the second model that led to its subsequent rejection.

The previous two instances of model construction both involved reasoning to construct causal models that can explain the clinical symptoms of the presenting case (hypothesis formulation) at the level of establishing what system or process was involved (i.e., the type and location of the lesion). Similar processes were found in the coach-initiated discussion in the third segment of the vascular theory (lines 123–151), in which the coach prompted Norman, Jenny, and Betty to identify more specific hypotheses concerning causes of the lesion through his question (see Figure 4): "So if it's vascular did he have a ↑stroke or is he having a TIA [transient ischemic attack]. What is the difference between those two things anyway?" (lines 123–127). What ensued was an elaboration of the TIA hypothesis

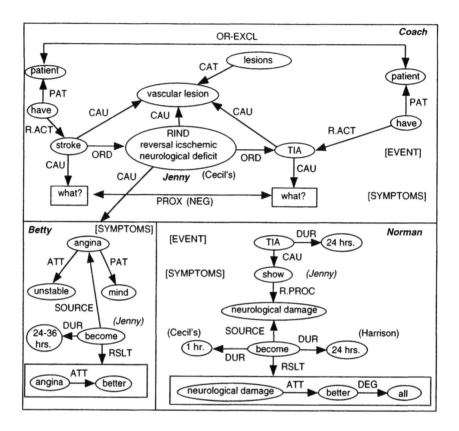

FIGURE 4 Collaborative construction of alternative explanatory hypotheses for the case.

by Norman ("With TIAs, it's like twenty-four hours," lines 128–129), an identification of some of its clinical effects by Jenny ("TIAs well, aʈccording to Harrison's TIAs um shows some neurological damage but it's all better in twenty-four hours. According to Cecil's it's all better in one hour," lines 130–134), and the introduction of a third hypothesis ("RI:ND [reversible ischemic neurological deficits]") and some of its clinical effects by Jenny (lines 136–151).

Collaborative Reasoning

To analyze the group's reasoning, we evaluated the *inferences* that relate each proposition introduced by a speaker to propositions that preceded it. The sequence of these inferences establishes the reasoning chain that the group produced to establish a differential diagnosis for the case. Our analysis of inferential links between propositions was similar to that of Patel and Groen (1991), which was based on a similar underlying model of propositional and conceptual network structures (Frederiksen, 1975, 1986; Patel, Groen, & Frederiksen, 1986). We were particularly interested in the direction of the reasoning because reasoning from causal hypotheses to clinical evidence may be attributable to the application of *backward, hypothesis-directed*, or *goal-driven* inference rules, whereas reasoning from clinical evidence to particular causes (i.e., hypotheses) is attributable to the application of *forward* or *data-driven* rules (Patel & Groen, 1991). In backward reasoning, a causal hypothesis is used to predict expected symptoms that are then tested against the available clinical evidence from the case; whereas in forward reasoning, the available clinical evidence from a case is used to identify a diagnostic hypothesis to account for the evidence (i.e., a cause that would be expected to lead to the observed symptoms). Forward reasoning has often been reported to be a characteristic of experienced diagnosticians solving routine diagnostic problems, whereas more complex mixed-reasoning strategies occur with novices or when experienced diagnosticians encounter loose ends (e.g., clinical facts that are inconsistent with a diagnostic explanation; Patel & Groen, 1993). In addition to this analysis of inferences, we compared the structure of this reasoning to a coding of the individual speech acts and conversational sequences that were produced by each of the speakers during their turns in the conversation. We were able to investigate in a preliminary way how the diagnostic reasoning process unfolded through conversational exchanges among the participants. A deeper analysis of the conversational structure would be required to explore more fully how the collaborative reasoning process was realized through the conversational structure of the dialogue and interactions among the participants (e.g., Fox, 1993; Heritage, 1984).

The results of these analyses are given in Figures 5 and 6. The discourse analyzed in Figure 5 consists of the group's reasoning to construct alternative diagnostic hypotheses; the dialogue analyzed in Figure 6 consists of reasoning involved in using the case evidence to evaluate these hypotheses. Line numbers in these figures correspond to lines in the "My Theory" dialogue transcript. Each line in the figures corresponds to a single conversational act (C-Act). The C-Act column gives a code based on Dore's (1980) model of C-Act types. A partial listing of some of these codes is given in the Appendix. In Dore's model, C-Acts combine according to conversational rules to form *requestive sequences* (initiated by a requestive and followed by one or more responses) and *nonrequestive sequences* (e.g., an assertive followed by an agreement or acknowledgment). In Figures 5 and 6, conversational sequences are represented by sequences of C-Act codes in boldface ending with an underline (indicating the end of the sequence). If a sequence was interrupted and subsequently continued, links are used to indicate where the sequence was resumed. Finally, the speaker is identified each time there is a speaker shift (i.e., a new turn in the conversation). The remaining two columns in Figures 5 and 6 correspond to the type of information about the case model that was expressed through the propositions: *Causal Hypotheses* and *Clinical Evidence*. In each column, there is a brief phrase (in parentheses) that summarizes the content of the propositions for the utterance. Any such phrases in the Clinical Evidence column that are in boldface

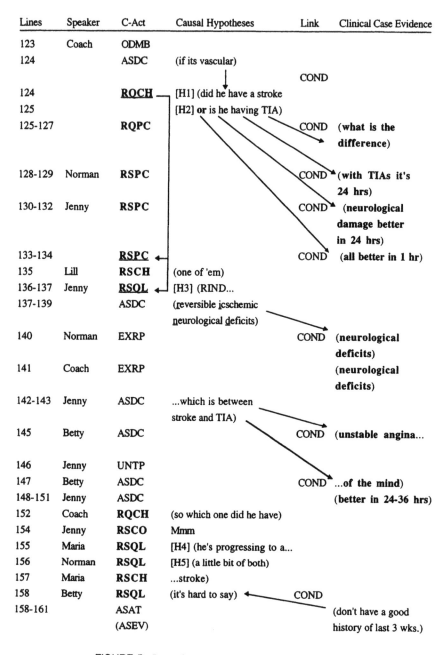

Lines	Speaker	C-Act	Causal Hypotheses	Link	Clinical Case Evidence
123	Coach	ODMB			
124		ASDC	(if its vascular)		
				COND	
124		**ROCH**	[H1] (did he have a stroke		
125			[H2] or is he having TIA)		
125-127		**RQPC**		COND	(what is the difference)
128-129	Norman	**RSPC**		COND	(with TIAs it's 24 hrs)
130-132	Jenny	**RSPC**		COND	(neurological damage better in 24 hrs)
133-134		**RSPC**		COND	(all better in 1 hr)
135	Lill	**RSCH**	(one of 'em)		
136-137	Jenny	**RSQL**	[H3] (RIND...		
137-139		ASDC	(reversible icschemic neurological deficits)		
140	Norman	EXRP		COND	(neurological deficits)
141	Coach	EXRP			(neurological deficits)
142-143	Jenny	ASDC	...which is between stroke and TIA)		
145	Betty	ASDC		COND	(unstable angina...
146	Jenny	UNTP			
147	Betty	ASDC		COND	...of the mind)
148-151	Jenny	ASDC			(better in 24-36 hrs)
152	Coach	**RQCH**	(so which one did he have)		
154	Jenny	RSCO	Mmm		
155	Maria	**RSQL**	[H4] (he's progressing to a...		
156	Norman	**RSQL**	[H5] (a little bit of both)		
157	Maria	RSCH	...stroke)		
158	Betty	**RSQL**	(it's hard to say)	COND	
158-161		ASAT (ASEV)			(don't have a good history of last 3 wks.)

FIGURE 5 Reasoning to construct diagnostic hypotheses.

type are *Expected Symptoms*; all others are symptoms reported as *Clinical Case Evidence*. The links in these two figures represent the conditional (COND) or causal (CAU) inferences that relate the propositions across these columns (i.e., that relate causal hypotheses to clinical evidence and vice versa). The direction of the link reflects the direction of the reasoning as expressed through the participants' discourse: It was either explicitly expressed or it was conveyed by the order in which propositions were introduced by the speakers. Links pointing from the Causal Hypotheses column to the Clinical Evidence column represent backward or hypothesis-directed inferences; links pointing in the opposite direction represent forward or data-driven inferences.

In Figure 5, lines 123–151 correspond to the conceptual model presented in Figure 4. Here, the coach introduced a shift in topic to procedure (3 1 1; i.e., "Formulate Hypotheses" in Figure 1). Then, reasoning from the premise that the lesion is vascular ("So if it's vascular," line 124), he introduced two causal hypotheses in the form of a choice question ("Did he have a ↑stroke or is he having a TIA?" lines 124–125). This question was immediately followed by a process question soliciting identification of clinical symptoms related to each ("What is the difference between those two things anyway?" lines 125–127). Norman responded to this question by specifying the expected duration of a TIA-related clinical symptom (lines 128–129), and then Jenny responded with statements about the expected time course of the resulting neurological damage (lines 130–134). Then, Lill (line 135) responded to the original (choice) question by restating the two alternatives, and Jenny responded to the same question by stating another hypothesis ("RI:ND," line 137) that provided an alternative account ("Which is somewhere in between a completed stroke and a TIA," lines 142–143) of the pattern of presenting symptoms. Other members of the group then proceeded to describe the expected clinical symptoms associated with RIND. In these exchanges, the reasoning was entirely a hypothesis-driven generation of expected symptoms.

Following this discussion, the coach set up the differential diagnosis problem by reintroducing his original question ("So which one did he ha:ve?" line 152) and directing the group away from consideration of Jenny's hypothesis. The coach's question led to two new hypotheses (about causes of the symptoms): Maria's hypothesis ("I think he's (.) progressing to a stroke," lines 155, 157) and Norman's hypothesis ("A little bit of both," line 156). The coach's question could have been answered with further inferences about causal models for the case or by proceeding to evaluate the two hypotheses against the case evidence. Here, Jenny and Maria responded to the coach's question with two new hypotheses about the causal model of the case, and then Betty qualified these responses with an expression of her uncertainty, which was a consequence of a lack of a good history of the patient over the past 3 weeks.

This led to a prolonged series of exchanges among the participants in which they reviewed the clinical evidence pertaining to the various diagnostic alterna-

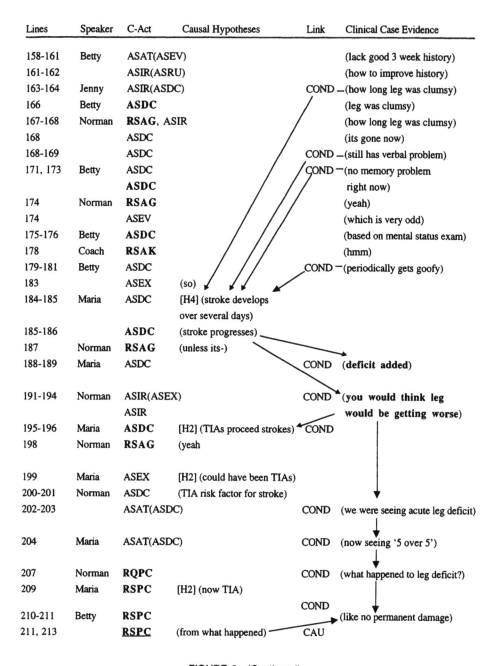

Lines	Speaker	C-Act	Causal Hypotheses	Link	Clinical Case Evidence
158-161	Betty	ASAT(ASEV)			(lack good 3 week history)
161-162		ASIR(ASRU)			(how to improve history)
163-164	Jenny	ASIR(ASDC)		COND	(how long leg was clumsy)
166	Betty	**ASDC**			(leg was clumsy)
167-168	Norman	**RSAG**, ASIR			(how long leg was clumsy)
168		ASDC			(its gone now)
168-169		ASDC		COND	(still has verbal problem)
171, 173	Betty	ASDC		COND	(no memory problem
		ASDC			right now)
174	Norman	**RSAG**			(yeah)
174		ASEV			(which is very odd)
175-176	Betty	**ASDC**			(based on mental status exam)
178	Coach	**RSAK**			(hmm)
179-181	Betty	ASDC		COND	(periodically gets goofy)
183		ASEX	(so)		
184-185	Maria	ASDC	[H4] (stroke develops		
			over several days)		
185-186		**ASDC**	(stroke progresses)		
187	Norman	**RSAG**	(unless its-)		
188-189	Maria	ASDC		COND	**(deficit added)**
191-194	Norman	ASIR(ASEX)		COND	**(you would think leg**
		ASIR			**would be getting worse)**
195-196	Maria	**ASDC**	[H2] (TIAs proceed strokes)	COND	
198	Norman	**RSAG**	(yeah		
199	Maria	ASEX	[H2] (could have been TIAs)		
200-201	Norman	ASDC	(TIA risk factor for stroke)		
202-203		ASAT(ASDC)		COND	(we were seeing acute leg deficit)
204	Maria	ASAT(ASDC)		COND	(now seeing '5 over 5')
207	Norman	**RQPC**		COND	(what happened to leg deficit?)
209	Maria	**RSPC**	[H2] (now TIA)		
				COND	
210-211	Betty	**RSPC**			(like no permanent damage)
211, 213		**<u>RSPC</u>**	(from what happened)	CAU	

FIGURE 6   (Continued)

152

Lines	Speaker	C-Act	Causal Hypotheses	Link	Clinical Case Evidence
214	Norman	**RQPC**	(why?) ────────▶	CAU	(speech screwed up)
216	Betty	**RSCL**, **RQCH**			(is it screwed up?)
217	Norman	**RSCH**			(it's screwed up)
218	Betty	**RSQL**			(a little bit)
219	Norman	**RSQL**			(it wasn't before)
220-221	Maria	**ASDC**			(speech gotten worse)
222	Norman	**RSAG**			(yeah)
223, 225	Maria	ASDC, ASIR			(speech has gotten worse)
224, 226-8	Betty	ASDC			(trouble finding right word)
228-231		ASDC			(finds words on mental exam)
231-232		ASDC		COND	(no other problems on exam)
234		ASIR	(I don't know)		
236-238		**ASIR**	[H6] (transient something)		
238-239		ASEX		COND	(catching him at good moment)
241	Maria	**RSAG?**			
242	Norman	**RSAG**			
243	Betty	ASEV	(don't know)		
245-248		ASEX			(has to be worse
				COND	(wife concerned)
249-250		ASAT(ASEV)		COND	(not a clear picture)
251		ASAT(ASEV)		COND	(things don't seem that bad)

FIGURE 6   Reasoning to evaluate clinical evidence and select a diagnostic hypothesis.

tives (lines 158–181), evaluated the hypotheses in relation to this evidence (lines 183–234, 243–248), and adopted the most plausible alternative based on their evaluation of the clinical evidence (lines 236–240). The analysis of these exchanges is given in Figure 6. First, a review of the clinical evidence was undertaken by Betty (lines 158–183), with Norman providing agreement responses to Betty's assertions and the coach providing one acknowledgment. Then, Maria entered the discussion (just as Betty started to give her explanation) with a data-driven (forward) inference in which she described a version of the stroke hypothesis that might be consistent with this evidence by elaborating it in a manner that emphasized its gradual and progressive course of development (lines 184–186, 188–189). Following Maria's elaboration of one expected consequence of the progressive stroke model ("A deficit being added from time to time," lines 188–189), Norman shifted the discussion to an evaluation of the stroke hypothesis by making a backward inference in which he asserted that the stroke model would imply clinical evidence that was contradictory with the observations (lines 191–194). A discussion ensued related to Norman's assertion (lines 195–213) consisting mostly of forward inferences by Maria in which she argued that the leg evidence suggested TIA as the cause (lines 195–196). These exchanges involved a dialogue between Norman and Maria in which Norman initially agreed with Maria (lines 198, 200–201), then returned to the (contradictory) leg findings, and finally raised a question: "What ↑happened to it [the leg deficit]?" (line 207). Following a weak attempt by Maria to reinstate the TIA hypothesis (line 209), Betty reentered the dialogue, concluding that there was no permanent damage from whatever had happened and directing the discussion back to the need for a data-driven consideration of the evidence and the current lack of an adequate explanation (lines 210–211, 213). Norman continued this line of reasoning, asking the more specific question: "Why is his ↑speech now screwed up?" (line 214). A discussion of the evidence related to the patient's speech followed. Betty then ended this discussion with a summary of the findings: that the speech has gotten worse but that there are no other problems on the mental exam. Betty then made her concluding evaluation of the evidence with two forward (data-driven) inferences leading to a fuzzy and uncertain hypothesis, that is, that the cause is uncertain (line 234) and that it is "something transient that comes'n goes" (lines 236–238). She followed this immediately with the (backward) inference that, in terms of his presenting symptoms, "we're catching him at a fairly good moment" (lines 238–239). Finally, she reiterated her uncertainty about the cause ("But I don't know," line 243) and her belief that it had to be worse given the evidence that was not clear (lines 245–251).

Contributions of Each Participant to the Discourse

Individuals differed in their contributions to the discourse and, by extension, in their contributions to clinical problem solving, to the construction of conceptual models of the case, and to the clinical reasoning process used to evaluate hypotheses against the clinical evidence. Furthermore, these differences appeared to be quite consistent for each individual. Although these differences are apparent in the previous analysis and discussion, it may be useful to summarize them from the standpoint of each participant. The coach had an important role in guiding the group's problem-solving actions, particularly through his prior knowledge and experience using the clinical inquiry procedure. This was apparent from the finding that, with the sole exception of Betty's expression of a preference for the vascular hypothesis in lines 116 and 119, it was the coach who initiated all discussions related to all the main procedures in the differential diagnosis frame (Figure 1). The coach shifted away from this guiding role once he had led the group to consider the clinical evidence and evaluate specific diagnostic hypotheses by setting up the differential diagnosis alternatives for consideration (Figure 1). The coach left the construction of case models mostly up to the students. However, the coach influenced this process first by asking a question challenging the space-occupying lesion model (that led Betty to abandon this model), and then by directly introducing two diagnostic hypotheses to the group to consider: stroke and TIA. By repeating his question, he led the group away from considering a

student-generated alternative: RIND. This directing of the clinical reasoning occurred despite the fact that the evidence was not clearly supportive of either
alternative (as the students discovered through their discussion of the case).

Betty had a prominent role in generating two hypotheses concerning the type
of lesion and its causes and effects: vascular or space-occupying lesion (Figures
2 and 3). Betty presented a general description of the vascular model from a
medical text and then proceeded to modify this model to make it appropriate to
the clinical case under consideration (Figure 2). She then presented the space-
occupying model and elaborated it in response to reactions from other students.
She finally abandoned it in response to the coach's question (Reaction 2, Figure
3). Betty also made important contributions to the group's clinical reasoning. In
the discussion provoked by the coach's second question, "So which one did he
ha:ve [stroke or TIA]?" (line 152), Betty entered the discussion of alternative
causes by highlighting the uncertainty of the cause given the lack of good evidence
(Figure 5). She then proceeded to summarize the evidence, leading the group to
consider whether the stroke or TIA models could account for the clinical evidence
(Figure 6). Finally, Betty entered this discussion by summarizing the clinical
findings and concluding with the fuzzy hypothesis that the cause is "something
transient" (line 237), that it is uncertain, and that the evidence is unclear. It is
also interesting that Betty consistently exhibited forward reasoning from clinical
evidence to a case model (hypothesis), and she also referred explicitly to the
causal connection between the hypothesis and the clinical symptoms.

Maria, Norman, and Jenny participated to varying degrees in the dialogue
through their reactions to Betty's theories and then in introducing their own
hypotheses. Maria contributed first through her reactions to Betty's other theory
(Figure 2) in which she identified consequences of a space-occupying lesion that
were inconsistent with the evidence. These led Betty to attempt to modify her
theory to account for these neurological and clinical consequences. In the subsequent clinical reasoning, Maria introduced her "hybrid" alternative model of a
progression from a TIA to a stroke (Figure 5) and persistently pursued this
hypothesis in her contributions to the evaluation of the stroke and TIA hypotheses
that followed (Figure 6). Prior to the coach's second question (line 152), Norman
contributed to the discussion mainly through responses to others that repeated or
added information. Following Maria's hypothesis, Norman added his own version
("A little bit of both," line 156; Figure 5). However, following Betty's summary
of the clinical evidence (Figure 6) and Maria's reintroduction of the stroke hypothesis, Norman shifted the discussion with a backward inference about the
evidence ("But then you would think the leg would [be] getting worse," lines
191–192). The following discussion with Maria and Betty included a requestive
sequence initiated by Norman with a question involving a backward inference
("Wh:y is his ↑speech now screwed up?" line 214). Norman appeared to focus
on aspects of the evidence that were suggested by particular causal hypotheses
(hypothesis-driven inferences) and on specific questions about the clinical evi-

dence. Finally, Jenny participated in model construction by elaborating on the time course of symptoms that follow a TIA event (Figure 4). She also introduced the RIND hypothesis (Figures 4 and 5). In the subsequent clinical reasoning, Jenny only participated once by expressing uncertainty about the time course of the clumsy leg symptom (lines 163–164). May and Lill did not participate at all in the diagnostic reasoning part of the dialogue. Lill's participation was limited to locating the hippocampus in one of the sections of the brain in the side sequence dealing with anatomy. Therefore, with this one exception, both May and Lill might be described as bystanders.

CONCLUSIONS

This analysis of the "My Theory" dialogue has shown how a particular interactive PBL discourse provided a variety of kinds of information and support for students learning to apply an inquiry procedure to solve diagnostic problems in medicine. Although these findings are necessarily limited to the particular PBL session and group that was studied, a number of conclusions seem warranted based on our data. They are offered as hypotheses for investigation in subsequent studies in other domains and with other PBL groups. First, the students were guided through a *general diagnostic inquiry procedure* by the coach. Through his interventions, the coach directed the students' discussion so that it would help them learn to use this inquiry procedure to guide their clinical reasoning and problem solving. The coach's interventions seemed designed to ensure that the discourse macrostructure, and hence the reasoning of the group, was disciplined in the sense that it was organized to reflect a coherent and general diagnostic inquiry procedure. Second, through its propositional content, the PBL discourse provided students with alternative conceptual models of the case and with a practical demonstration of the cognitive processes by which explanatory case models are constructed using clinical information and biomedical knowledge. Because the discourse was coconstructed by the members of the group, it also enabled them to participate in the process of constructing these explanatory case models. Thus, the discourse provided the students with an opportunity to engage in a process of *collaborative knowledge building* to develop and evaluate alternative case models in a realistic professional context. Third, differential diagnosis (the generation and comparison of alternative diagnostic models) was achieved through a procedurally guided *interactive reasoning process* in which (a) alternative case models and specific diagnostic hypotheses were constructed, (b) the available clinical evidence was reviewed and evaluated, and (c) diagnostic hypotheses were evaluated against the clinical evidence. This reasoning process involved both backward inferences (from hypotheses to identify the expected clinical evidence) and forward reasoning (from clinical case evidence to suggest particular causal hypotheses to account for the evidence). This complex combination of hypothesis-directed and data-driven inference suggests that students were reasoning in different ways, sometimes from hypothesis to data (a direction commonly reported as typical of novices) and sometimes from data to hypotheses (frequently associated with experts' diagnostic reasoning for routine cases). This exposure to mixed-reasoning strategies may be advantageous in helping students learn to reason in a variety of ways before they have acquired sufficient knowledge of clinical cases to adhere to more expert reasoning strategies. The patterns of this reasoning reflect both the reasoning of individuals and patterns of interaction among the participants through the dialogue. The conversational structure of this dialogue provides a framework to motivate local conversational exchanges and thus help maintain the reasoning process throughout the discourse. The coach's interventions served to steer the direction of this reasoning dialogue so that it focused on particular models of the case. Finally, individuals in this PBL group differed greatly in their contributions to the group's discourse. For bystanders (i.e., those who did not participate or who participated only minimally in the discussion of the case), the discourse supported their learning by providing them with exposure to biomedical and clinical knowledge and to a demonstration of how this particular group attempted to apply it to solve a diagnostic problem. Despite the fact that the clinical reasoning process was that of a group of students rather than a group of experts, the coach's interventions ensured that the group's reasoning was organized to reflect a coherent method of diagnostic inquiry; that is, that it covered all of the steps in the inquiry procedure that experts use to arrive at a differential diagnosis. For members of the group who contributed actively to this clinical reasoning process through their contributions to the dialogue, the PBL group gave them the opportunity to participate in a reasoning process that included a mixture of forward and backward inferences. The interactive structure of the group's dialogue enabled these individuals to engage in a clinical reasoning process without having to be able to maintain the process independently. Thus, active participants in the dialogue were offered an opportunity to engage in solving difficult and realistic diagnostic problems with the guidance and assistance of a coach at an early stage in their learning.

These results are consistent with a cognitive theory of cooperative PBL that incorporates levels of cognitive representation and processing that have been identified in current models of learning from text or discourse. Specifically, they demonstrate that a multilevel model of the cognitive representation and processing of discourse can be applied to the study of learning through interactive, task-oriented dialogue in realistic contexts of collaborative reasoning and problem solving. Through its content, discourse in a PBL group strongly supports and constrains students' cognitive processing by exposing them to biomedical and clinical knowledge and to demonstrations of how to apply this knowledge to solve diagnostic problems. The discourse that is coconstructed by the members of a PBL group enables them to collaborate in constructing explanatory models for clinical cases and, through its local microstructure (e.g., local inferences and reasoning chains) and its macrostructure (e.g., the inquiry procedure frame and the structure of biomedical knowledge in the domain), the PBL discourse provides both local and global frameworks to guide and constrain the students' ongoing reasoning and problem-solving activity. In addition, these local and global constraints on students' cognitive processing are strongly reinforced by the conversational structure of the dialogue, by the social organization of the group, and by the participation structure of the group's conversational and collaborative activity. In this way, the social structure of the PBL dialogue supports and complements the group's collaborative cognitive processes of meaning construction, reasoning, and problem solving. Thus, the social obligation to participate in the group's discussion powerfully supports participation and involvement in complex knowledge construction and problem-solving processes.

This discourse analysis has shown how the content of task-oriented dialogue in a PBL group is embedded in the social structure of interaction and cooperative problem-solving activity within the group. It also has identified some of the ways in which the discourse that is produced in such groups supports and constrains students' construction of knowledge and development of cognitive and socio-cognitive expertise. Ultimately, the study of these complex learning processes requires theoretical perspectives and analysis tools from multiple disciplines (Duranti & Goodwin, 1992). Analyses from a cognitive perspective are needed to uncover the knowledge structures and cognitive processes underlying construction of case models, reasoning, and problem solving within the group, and deeper analyses of social interaction and conversational structure are needed to understand how these cognitive processes are framed by the social interaction and participation structure of the group and by the structure of conversational exchanges and inferences within the group (Fox, 1993; Gumperz, 1992; Heritage, 1984; Tannen, 1993). A comparison of the results reported here with analyses of "My Theory" from other theoretical perspectives should begin to reveal the enormous potential of a multidisciplinary approach to modeling human learning, both as a cognitive and as a sociocognitive process.

ACKNOWLEDGMENTS

I thank Walter Kintsch, Rogers Hall, and Phillip Glenn for their helpful comments on an earlier version of this article, and I thank Lorraine Meilleur for her editorial assistance with the preparation of the manuscript. The complete analysis of the transcript is available at http://www.education.mcgill.ca/acsrg/

REFERENCES

Barrows, H. S. (1985). *How to design a problem-based curriculum for the preclinical years*. New York: Springer-Verlag.

Barrows, H. S. (1986). A taxonomy of problem-based learning methods. *Medical Education, 20,* 481–486.

Barrows, H. S., & Feltovich, P. J. (1987). The clinical reasoning process. *Journal of Medical Education, 21,* 86–91.

Barrows, H. S., & Tamblyn, R. (1980). *Problem-based learning: An approach to medical education.* New York: Springer.

Brown, J. S., Collins, A., & Duguid, P. (1989). Situated cognition and the culture of learning. *Educational Researcher, 18*(1), 32–42.

Collins, A., Brown, J. S., & Newman, S. E. (1989). Cognitive apprenticeship: Teaching the crafts of reading, writing, and mathematics. In L. B. Resnick (Ed.), *Knowing, learning and instruction: Essays in honor of Robert Glaser* (pp. 453–494). Hillsdale, NJ: Lawrence Erlbaum Associates, Inc.

Dore, J. (1980). Conversation and preschool language development. In P. Fletcher & M. Carman (Eds.), *Language acquisition: Studies in first language development* (pp. 337–361). New York: Cambridge University Press.

Duranti, A., & Goodwin, C. (1992). *Rethinking context: Language as an interactive phenomenon.* New York: Cambridge University Press.

Fox, B. A. (1993). *The human tutorial dialogue project: Issues in the design of instructional systems.* Hillsdale, NJ: Lawrence Erlbaum Associates, Inc.

Frederiksen, C. H. (1975). Representing logical and semantic structure of knowledge acquired from discourse. *Cognitive Psychology, 7,* 371–458.

Frederiksen, C. H. (1986). Cognitive models and discourse analysis. In C. R. Cooper & S. Greenbaum (Eds.), *Written communication annual: Vol. 1. Studying writing: Linguistic approaches* (pp. 227–267). Beverly Hills, CA: Sage.

Frederiksen, C. H., & Breuleux, A. (1990). Monitoring cognitive processing in semantically complex domains. In N. Frederiksen, R. Glaser, A. Lesgold, & M. Shafto (Eds.), *Diagnostic monitoring of skill and knowledge acquisition* (pp. 351–391). Hillsdale, NJ: Lawrence Erlbaum Associates, Inc.

Frederiksen, C. H., & Donin, J. D. (1991). Constructing multiple semantic representations in comprehending and producing discourse. In G. Denhière & J. -P. Rossi (Eds.), *Text and text processing* (pp. 19–44). Amsterdam: Elsevier.

Frederiksen, C. H., & Emond, B. (1993). La représentation et le traitement cognitif du discours: Le rôle des modèles formels [The representation and cognitive processing of discourse: The role of formal models]. In J. -F. Le Ny (Ed.), *Intelligence naturelle et artificielle* (pp. 165–195). Paris: Presse Universitaire de France.

Gumperz, J. (1992). Contextualization in understanding. In A. Duranti & C. Goodwin (Eds.), *Rethinking context: Language as an interactive phenomenon* (pp. 229–252). Cambridge, England: Cambridge University Press.

Heritage, J. (1984). *Garfinkel and ethnomethodology.* Cambridge, MA: Blackwell.

Kintsch, W. (1991). The role of knowledge in discourse comprehension: A construction–integration model. In G. Denhière & J. -P. Rossi (Eds.), *Text and text processing* (pp. 107–153). Amsterdam: Elsevier.

Koschmann, T. D., Myers, A. C., Feltovich, P. J., & Barrows, H. S. (1993–1994). Using technology to assist in realizing effective learning and instruction: A principled approach to the use of computers in collaborative learning. *The Journal of the Learning Sciences, 3,* 227–264.

Patel, V. L., & Groen, G. (1991). The general and specific nature of medical expertise: A critical look. In K. A. Ericsson & J. Smith (Eds.), *Toward a general theory of expertise: Prospects and limits* (pp. 91–116). New York: Cambridge University Press.

Patel, V. L., & Groen, G. (1993). Comparing apples and oranges: Some dangers in confusing frameworks with theories. *Cognitive Science, 17,* 135–141.

Patel, V. L., Groen, G., & Frederiksen, C. H. (1986). Differences between students and physicians in memory for clinical cases. *Medical Education, 20,* 3–9.

Sowa, J. F. (1983). *Conceptual structures: Information processing in mind and machine.* Reading, MA: Addison-Wesley.

Tannen, D. (1993). What's in a frame? Surface evidence for underlying expectations. In D. Tannen (Ed.), *Framing in discourse* (pp. 15–55). New York: Oxford University Press.

van Dijk, T. A. M., & Kintsch, W. (1983). *Strategies of discourse comprehension.* New York: Academic.

APPENDIX

According to Dore's (1980) model, conversational acts (C-Acts) are units of conversational dialogue that satisfy a particular function within the conversation (i.e., they correspond to particular uses of language within the interactive context of the conversation). C-Acts may be used to solicit (i.e., *request*) information or actions from another participant in a conversation (e.g., choice questions [RQCH], product questions [RQPD], process questions [RQPC], action requests [RQAC], permission requests [RQPM], suggestions [RQSU]); they may be used to *respond* to such solicitations (e.g., choice responses [RSCH], process responses [RSPC], compliance responses expressing acceptance, denial, or acknowledgment of a prior request [RSCO], and qualification responses that provide unsolicited information to a request [RSQL]; they may be used to *regulate* the flow of a conversation and support participation by others in the conversation and activity (e.g., boundary markers [ODBM], questions seeking clarification of prior C-Acts [ODCQ]); and they may *assert* propositional information for acceptance by other participants (e.g., assert a description of a situation or relevant prior knowledge [ASDC], assert an evaluation or express a personal judgment or attitude [ASEV]). In addition, they may respond to nonrequestive speech acts by *acknowledging* reception of a prior nonrequestive (RSAK) or conveying *agreement* or *disagreement* (RSAG). *Expressive* speech acts may nonpropositionally express attitudes or affective reactions (EXCL), they may accompany an action providing information that is redundant with the action or its context (EXAC), or they may repeat prior utterances (EXRP). Finally, *performative* speech acts may accomplish (i.e., perform) actions through the utterances themselves (e.g., jokes [PFJO], claims [PFCL], protests [PFPR]).

DISCOURSE PROCESSES, 27(2), 161–171

Applying a Sociocultural Lens to the Work of a Transition Community

Annemarie Sullivan Palincsar

Literacy, Language, and Learning Disabilities
School of Education
University of Michigan

Drawing on Bruffee's (1993) notion of transition communities, this article examines the video excerpt for evidence of the ways in which the participants constitute a discourse community in the process of reacculturation into the medical community they aspire to join. Specifically, the article explores several features of transition communities and considers the challenges these features pose for others interested in the design and analysis of transition communities. These features include (a) the multiple agendas confronting a transition community, (b) the intra- and interpersonal issues, and (c) the role of the coach in transition communities.

In her remarkable book entitled, *The Anatomy of Judgment,* Minnie Johnson Abercrombie (1960) observed:

> Discussion in a group does for thinking what testing on real objects does for seeing. We become aware of discrepancies between different people's interpretations of the same stimulus and are driven to weigh the evidence in favor of alternative interpretations. . . . The aim of free group discussion is to help the individual participant reach a better understanding of the factors that affect scientific judgments in order to secure better control over them so they can make sounder judgments. (p. 62)

In this text, Abercrombie reflected on her experiences as a professor in the Department of Anatomy at University College, London, where she participated in the preparation of medical students. Her decision to depart from didactic pedagogy in favor of group discussions was influenced by observations regarding the problems of medical education. As a report of the Royal College of Physicians

Correspondence and requests for reprints should be sent to Annemarie Sullivan Palincsar, Literacy, Language, and Learning Disabilities, University of Michigan, 4204C School of Education, 610 East University, Ann Arbor, MI 48109–1259. E-mail: annemari@umich.edu

concluded: "The average medical graduate tends to lack curiosity and initiative; his powers of observation are relatively underdeveloped; his ability to arrange and interpret facts is poor; he lacks precision in the use of words" (as cited in Abercrombie, 1960, pp. 15–16). Although Abercrombie did her work in the 1950s, she anticipates contemporary interest in the role of social interaction in cognition and in the significance of elaboration, interpretation, explanation, and argumentation in promoting learning.

SOCIAL PROCESSES OF LEARNING

The role of social processes as a mechanism for learning is usually identified with Vygotsky, who suggested: "The social dimension of consciousness is primary in time and in fact. The individual dimension of consciousness is derivative and secondary" (as cited in Wertsch & Bivens, 1992, p. 35). From this perspective, mental functioning of the individual is not simply derived from social interaction; rather, the specific structures and processes revealed by individuals can be traced to their interactions with others. Furthermore, from a sociocultural perspective, cognition itself is a collaborative process (see Rogoff, 1998), and the purpose of inquiry regarding cognitive development is to examine the transformation of socially shared activities into internalized processes (see John-Steiner & Mahn, 1996). Wertsch (1991) proposed three major themes in Vygotsky's writings that elucidate the nature of the interdependence between individual and social processes in the coconstruction of knowledge.

The first theme is that individual development, including higher mental functioning, has its origins in social sources. This theme is best represented in Vygotsky's "genetic law of development":

> Every function in the cultural development of the child comes on the stage twice, in two respects: first in the social, later in the psychological, first in relations between people as an interpsychological category, afterwards within the child as an intrapsychological category. . . . All higher psychological functions are internalized relationships of the social kind, and constitute the social structure of personality. (as cited in Valsiner, 1987, p. 67)

From this perspective, as learners participate in a broad range of joint activities and internalize the effects of working together, they acquire new strategies and knowledge of the world and culture. Typically, this tenet has been illustrated examining the interactions of more and less knowledgeable others, for example, children and their caregivers or experts and novices. However, these illustrations may be misleading to the extent that they suggest a transmission process when, in fact, it is equally interesting to explore the processes of coconstruction, transaction, and transformation when considering the means by which this internalization process occurs. For example, the article by Glenn, Koschmann, and Conlee (1999/this issue) explores the interplay of various actions such as generating claims, requesting clarifying information, and providing both fitting as well as conflicting evidence, in assessing and coconstructing a theory.

The second Vygotskian theme that Wertsch (1991) identified is that human action, on both the social and individual planes, is mediated by tools and signs—semiotics. The semiotic means include "language; various systems of counting; mnemonic techniques; algebraic symbol systems; works of art; writing; schemes, diagrams, maps and mechanical drawings; all sorts of conventional signs and so on" (Vygotsky, 1981, p. 147). These semiotic means are both the tools that facilitate the coconstruction of knowledge and the means that are internalized or appropriated (Leont'ev, 1981) to aid future independent problem-solving activity. It is in this sense that the process of collaboration is at the same time the product of collaboration. The article by Lemke (1999/this issue) examines two semiotic means that are salient in this excerpt: topological and typological reasoning.

The third theme that Wertsch (1991) proposed from Vygotsky's writing is that the first two themes are best examined through genetic, or developmental, analysis:

> To study something historically means to study it in the process of change; that is the dialectical method's basic demand. To encompass in research the process of a given thing's development in all its phases and changes—from birth to death—fundamentally means to discover its nature, its essence, for it is only in movement that a body shows what it is. Thus the historical study of behavior is not an auxiliary aspect of theoretical study, but rather forms its very base. (Vygotsky, 1978, pp. 64–65)

In summary, from a sociocultural perspective, learning and development take place in socially and culturally shaped contexts, which are themselves constantly changing; there can be no universal scheme that adequately represents the dynamic interaction between the external and internal aspects of development. There is no generic development that is independent of communities and their practices. Hence, it is with the use of genetic analysis that the complex interplay of mediational tools, the individual, and the social world is explored to understand the processes of learning and development as well as the transformation of tools, practices, and institutions. Virtually every article in this special issue illustrates some form of genetic analysis.

This sociocultural perspective, in hand with evolving constructivist views of the learner, has had an enormous impact on educational research and practice. Although the knowledge base regarding the role of social processes in enhancing cognition is significant (see Webb & Palincsar, 1996), there are a number of thorny issues that remain to be examined regarding collaborative problem-solving contexts. One of the most interesting challenges offered by the sociocultural perspective is to engage in analysis in a manner that reflects the interplay of cognitive, social, motivational, emotional, and identity processes. I would like to use the Southern Illinois University video excerpt of medical students engaged in problem-based learning (PBL) to illustrate this kind of analysis. I begin by describing a particular framework for characterizing the nature of this group.

TRANSITION COMMUNITIES

Bruffee (1993) proposed the term *transition communities* to characterize discourse communities that are made up of people who are reacculturating themselves into the knowledge communities they aspire to join. Reflecting a sociocultural perspective, Bruffee argued that it is through participation in discourse communities that individuals can acquire and refine the language, ways of reasoning, and tools of the new community to which they aspire. In this video excerpt, we see the interactions of one such transition community—a group of students "trying on" the discourse and semiotic means of the medical community.

There are different formulations as to what constitutes a discourse community. Kent (1991) noted that discourse communities can be depicted along a continuum from *thick formulations,* in which the community is described as a system of social conventions that may be isolated and codified (as in a disciplinary community in which there are distinct intellectual and social conventions) to *thin formulations,* in which there is a relatively indeterminate and uncodifiable collection of voices expressing an array of beliefs and desires. In this article, I employ the full range of the continuum to the extent of describing a group that moves its way back and forth along this continuum.

Specifically, this article explores what the video excerpts reveal about several features of transition communities and the challenges these features pose for those of us who are interested in the design and analysis of transition communities from a sociocultural perspective.[1] However, the analysis must begin with a caveat indicating that a considerable amount of speculation is necessary in this exploration because the excerpt offers but a brief glimpse (6 min) into the life of this group, I was not present for the exchanges of this group, and none of the participants were informants in this analysis. Nevertheless, the video excerpts are provocative to the extent that they raise issues regarding interpersonal, personal, and contextual aspects of PBL groups that command the attention of educators. In my analysis of the interpersonal dimension, I speak to the nature of dual agendas that operate in transition communities and are reflected interpersonally. The personal issue that I explore is one of identity in learning and development. Finally, the contextual issue that I examine is the role of the coach in this transition community.

---

[1]My thinking about transition communities has been very influenced by the research that my colleague, Andy Anderson at Michigan State University, and I have been engaged in with sixth-grade students involved in collaborative problem solving in science.

Goodnow (1993), among others, criticized sociocultural approaches to teaching and learning for their benign views of the motivations of participants in a learning community. Those of us who design these kinds of learning environments want to think that there are positive alliances within the group and that the individuals within the group are working to help one another toward clearer understandings. The group, it is purported, does this when members challenge each other's thinking, help others to discover their unexamined assumptions, or work in constructive ways to extend one another's ideas. We want to believe that students learn to "develop authority relative to one another, acknowledge one another's authority, and accept authority themselves relative to their peers when it's appropriate and helpful" (K. Bruffee, personal communication, April 29, 1996).

Although these are worthy aspirations for a group, groups do not always interact in this fashion. As Tannen (1996) pointed out in her research, interactions among people are inevitably occasions when they pursue dual agendas based on deep personal needs. We all need a sense of power or status on one hand and a sense of solidarity or interpersonal connection on the other. These dual agendas are always present among transition communities. The exchange initiated by Betty may be illustrative of this phenomenon.

The exchange begins with Betty's statement on line 69, "My other theory is . . ." She makes a 58-word utterance, which is actually quite long in comparison with the mean length of the utterances of her colleagues. The group reaction is interesting at that point; there is some laughter, her statement clearly causes a stir, and the coach actually says, "Whoa kay" (line 81). What I found intriguing is that, in her next utterance (beginning on line 86), Betty seems to reign in her fluency. In an uncharacteristic fashion, she falters "somato:graphic whatever that word was, (.)"

This event might not have caught my attention if it were not for the fact that it mirrored patterns of interaction that we have seen in our work with sixth-grade students (Kurth, Anderson, & Palincsar, 1995), especially very competent sixth-grade girls who seem to hold back and are very tentative in their contributions. These interactions have led us to consider the ways in which transitional communities are first human communities, complete with their own conventions and histories of interpersonal relationships. This issue can be explored in several ways. For example, one wonders if Betty's drawing back (beginning on line 86) was not a move that would prevent her from straying too far from the conventions and discourse patterns of the group and would affirm her solidarity with group members.

There is now sufficient evidence in the research literature on collaborative learning that the kinds of interactions that give rise to learning in a community, including challenging one another's ideas and presenting counterevidence to undermine an argument (cf. Chan, Burtis, & Bereiter, 1997; Cobb, Wood, & Yackel, 1993), are the very kinds of interactions that can threaten or erode social coherence and trust. These kinds of productive interactions are dependent on experiencing social coherence and trust. The challenge, then, is to attend to both the intellectual and interpersonal dimensions of the transition group's activity. The risk of failure to do this is that students' interpersonal agendas can usurp the problem-solving activity (examples include arguments that become explicitly personal rather than based on theory and evidence) or that low-status students can be marginalized and effectively excluded from the transition community (cf. Anderson, Holland, & Palincsar, 1997; Kurth et al., 1995; O'Connor, 1996).

Although these interpersonal issues merit attention when considering the development of a transition community, there are also personal or individual issues. One set of such issues has to do with the variation among the participants in terms of their "place" in the transition process. This is a complex issue in the collaborative problem-solving literature and can be characterized in cognitive terms, social status terms, and identity terms. With regard to the cognitive issues, on one hand, one can argue that, if the participants shared the same knowledge and perspective, much of the potential power of the process would be lost to a sense of complacency or stagnation. On the other hand, we know relatively little about what constitutes optimum variability and how to most appropriately exploit this variability. For example, Bell, Grossen, and Perret-Clermont (1985) determined that children working with peers showed more cognitive growth than children working alone; however, this was true only when each of the partners was actively engaged in the problem-solving activity. Furthermore, if one partner's cognitive level was too far in advance of the other's, the partner's answers were simply accepted and did not stimulate problem-solving efforts on behalf of the second child. Similar findings are reported by Chan et al. (1997) and by Webb and Farivar (1999) in their work with adolescents.

Adding to this complexity is the issue of social dominance. Research conducted by Russell, Mills, and Reiff-Musgrove (1990) suggests that social dominance influenced whether one learner's answer was adopted by another learner in a paired learning situation; having the right answer was not always enough to persuade the other participant. Similar findings are reported by O'Connor (1996).

A third personal issue that might be especially germane in this context is related to the possible role that identity plays in the positions of these community members. Lave and Wenger (1991) explained: "Learning involves the whole person. It implies not only a relation to specific activities, but a relation to social communities. Learning is becoming a different person with respect to the possibilities enabled by these systems of relations" (p. 53). They warned that to ignore this aspect of learning is to overlook the fact that learning involves the construction of identities, ways of understanding and viewing oneself and being viewed by others. Another reason to consider the issue of identity is that these communities work when all members can productively engage in the discourse, and as Bakhtin (1981) suggested, active engagement occurs only if individuals "populate the discourse" with their own interests, desires, and purposes.

The variations in the identities and changing identities of community members can be explored in several ways. For example, the knowledge or discourse communities in which these members have previously participated will likely position the participants differently in this transition community. Students who are more familiar with evidence-based argumentation, perhaps through advanced science classes, are likely to be more comfortable in these exchanges, more inclined to support their own positions, and less likely to acquiesce to others. In this particular exchange, Norman and Betty offer interesting contrasts. The regularity with which Norman joins in on the exchange suggests that he is clearly engaged in the problem-solving activity. However, the nature of his contributions suggests that his engagement is significantly scaffolded by the other participants. For example, his utterances are often in the form of affirmations (e.g., lines 42, 84, and 102). The majority of his other utterances are echoes of his colleagues' utterances (e.g., 15, 62, 99, 115, and 140). Interestingly, it is not until line 169 that Norman seeds the conversation with a new consideration, as he notes that the patient still has the "verbal problem."

Norman's mode of participation stands in stark contrast to Betty's. From the beginning, Betty is taking the most significant risks in the dialogue, speaking in complete sentences, and offering more grist for the discussion than all of the other members of the group combined, including her introduction of the interesting metaphor, "angina or unstable angina of the mind" (lines 145, 147). The intriguing questions begged by these contrasts include the extent to which Betty's contributions are advancing the ability of the entire group to engage in this problem-solving activity or the extent to which it is possible that her fluency discourages the participation of others or leaves the coach with misconceptions about the state of understanding of the group as a whole.

For some of the participants in this particular transition community, their identity as a member of the community of medical practice seems quite emergent; for others, it appears more well developed. For example, in response to the coach's question regarding the difference between a TIA (transient ischemic attack) and a stroke, Jenny tentatively quotes from two medical texts, concluding with "I don't know" (line 151). Betty, in contrast, seems more ready to assume the identity of the discourse community to which she aspires. She is comfortable claiming twice that she has a theory. There is even a point when Betty inquires, "But yet his wife says" (line 179), demonstrating how alive the case text is for her. But what about the young woman at the end of the table (i.e., Lill) who makes neither verbal nor nonverbal contributions to the group? What is her participation in this community? I wondered how clearly she was able to imagine a possible self (drawing on Marcus & Nurius, 1986) in which she was a productive, well-received member in a community of medical practice? Of course, one has to be careful drawing conclusions about talking as the only means of participating or contributing to the group's activity, but it seems worth considering whether this member of the group is challenged in a manner that others in the group are not challenged.

This means that, in addition to the cognitive, linguistic, and interpersonal challenges faced by members of a transitional community, there are the challenges inherent in giving up the identity with which one has attained some degree of comfort and negotiating a different identity. My colleague, Jean McPhail, has studied this phenomenon among medical students from underrepresented groups and has illustrated the powerful role that identity issues assume in explaining both the successes and failures of these medical school students (McPhail, 1996).

A second issue that is illustrated effectively in this excerpt is the role of more expert others in assisting transition community members in negotiating their way into the new community. Rorty (1979) described "conversation at community boundaries" in which the participants do not yet agree on the conventions that will guide their conversations, do not yet agree on how to evaluate what another person says, and are unsure as to what counts as a relevant contribution or a satisfactory answer, a good argument, or a good criticism of the argument.

The coach in this transition community has the potential to play numerous roles that can promote a culture in which the participants are validators of one another's ideas, including establishing norms such as persisting in the solution of personally challenging problems, explaining personal solutions, listening to and striving to make sense of other's contributions, and working to achieve consensus regarding the problem and the solution process.

This feature is illustrated in the targeted segment by considering the pivotal role that the coach plays in the exchange among the group. Throughout the exchange, the coach seeds the conversations at important junctures, enabling the group to proceed. For example, four of the participants in lines 17–31 are offering their conjectures as to the location of the hippocampus when the coach, in line 33, helps the group find an appropriate view in which to find the hippocampus. Similarly, in line 104, when the students are jointly constructing an argument in favor of a space-occupying lesion, it is the coach who provides the counterevidence that would need to be explained to support this particular argument (i.e., "So why do the leg findings go away?"). In lines 124–126, the coach plays a pivotal role in modeling the process of building an argument when he urges the students to consider the differences between a stroke and a TIA as a means of evaluating the evidence in favor of one or the other diagnosis. Finally, as the dialogue bogs down and approaches a near standstill around line 152, it is the coach who breathes new life into the conversation with his question, "So which one did he ha:ve?"

There is enormous skill required on the part of a coach in this conversation, illustrating an area ripe for research: How does one support a community "on the boundary?" This coach makes relatively few verbalizations compared to the other participants; however, his contributions come at key points in the conversation and appear to play a critical role in advancing the inquiry. Indeed, the analysis that Taylor and Cox (1997) conducted regarding the interactions of tutors and tutees determined that the support of the tutor was not a function of the number of statements made but rather that the statements came at the right time when they would indeed scaffold learning.

CONCLUSIONS

The opportunity that this particular forum has provided for examining collaborative problem solving from multiple perspectives is enormously exciting. The past two decades of research on group processes have revealed the myriad complexities operating in group contexts. The type of inquiry generated in this project serves to illustrate how bringing multiple perspectives to bear can aid our understanding of these issues while maintaining their complexity.

Historically, research on small-group learning has examined the development of skills and rather simple concepts. The focus on clinical reasoning, featured in this exchange, is a productive focus that should serve to inform the knowledge base regarding collaborative learning in significant ways. For example, this research can inform us about productively scaffolding groups' interaction in terms of the nature of the case, the role of various semiotic means in supporting the problem-solving endeavor (case history materials, photos, source books, etc.), and the roles of more knowledgeable others, such as coaches and medical experts, in supporting the group's efforts.

Finally, the sociocultural perspective offers a particularly useful lens with which to investigate and understand the processes and outcomes of collaborative learning in PBL contexts.

ACKNOWLEDGMENTS

I acknowledge the helpful comments of Kenneth Bruffee, James Gee, Jay Lemke, Carl Frederiksen, and Tim Koschmann, who reviewed an earlier draft of this article.

REFERENCES

Abercrombie, M. L. J. (1960). *Anatomy of judgment.* London: Hutchinson.
Anderson, C. A., Holland, D., & Palincsar, A. S. (1997). Canonical and sociocultural approaches to research and reform in science education. *Elementary School Journal, 97,* 357–381.
Bakhtin, M. (1981). *The dialogic imagination.* Austin: University of Texas Press.
Bell, N., Grossen, M., & Perret-Clermont, A. -N. (1985). Sociocognitive conflict and intellectual growth. In M. W. Berkowitz (Ed.), *Peer conflict and psychological growth* (pp. 41–54). San Francisco: Jossey-Bass.

Bruffee, K. A. (1993). *Collaborative learning: Higher education, interdependence and the authority of knowledge*. Baltimore: Johns Hopkins University Press.

Chan, C., Burtis, J., & Bereiter, C. (1997). Knowledge building as a mediator of conflict in conceptual change. *Cognition and Instruction, 15*, 1–40.

Cobb, P., Wood, T., & Yackel, E. (1993). Discourse, mathematical thinking, and classroom practice. In E. D. Forman, N. Minick, & C. A. Stone (Eds.), *Contexts for learning* (pp. 91–119). New York: Oxford University Press.

Glenn, P. J., Koschmann, T., & Conlee, M. (1999/this issue). Theory presentation and assessment in a problem-based learning group. *Discourse Processes, 27*, 119–133.

Goodnow, J. J. (1993). Direction of post-Vygotskian research. In E. A. Forman, N. Minick, & C. A. Stone (Eds.), *Contexts for learning: Sociocultural dynamics in children's development* (pp. 369–382). New York: Oxford University Press.

John-Steiner, V., & Mahn, H. (1996). Sociocultural approaches to learning and development: A Vygotskian framework. *Educational Psychologist, 31*, 191–206.

Kent, T. (1991). On the very idea of a discourse community. *College Composition and Communication, 42*, 425–445.

Kurth, L., Anderson, C. A., & Palincsar, A. S. (1995, April). *Pursuing multiple reform agendas in middle school science teaching*. Paper presented at the annual meeting of the National Association for Research in Science Teaching, San Francisco.

Lave, J., & Wenger, E. (1991). *Situated learning: Legitimate peripheral participation*. Cambridge, England: Cambridge University Press.

Lemke, J. L. (1999/this issue). Typological and topological meaning in diagnostic discourse. *Discourse Processes, 27*, 173–185.

Leont'ev, A. N. (1981). *Problems of the development of mind*. Moscow, Russia: Moscow Progress Press.

Marcus, H., & Nurius, P. (1986). Possible selves. *American Psychologist, 41*, 954–969.

McPhail, J. (1996, April). *Genuine interest in becoming a physician: Two stories, two lives*. Paper presented at the annual meeting of the American Educational Research Association, New York.

O'Connor, M. C. (1996). Managing the intermental: Classroom group discussion and the social context of learning. In D. I. Slobin, J. Gerhardt, A. Kyratzis, & J. Guo (Eds.), *Social interaction, social context, and language: Essays in honor of Susan Ervin-Tripp* (pp. 495–509). Mahwah, NJ: Lawrence Erlbaum Associates, Inc.

Rogoff, B. (1998). Cognition as a collaborative process. In W. Damon (Series Ed.) & R. S. Siegler & D. Kuhn (Eds.), *Handbook of child psychology: Vol. 2. Cognitive, language, and perceptual development* (pp. 679–744). New York: Wiley.

Rorty, R. (1979). *Philosophy and the mirror of nature*. Princeton, NJ: Princeton University Press.

Russell, J., Mills, I., & Reiff-Musgrove, P. (1990). The role of symmetrical and asymmetrical social conflict in cognitive change. *Journal of Experimental Child Psychology, 49*, 58–78.

Tannen, D. (1996). *Gender & discourse*. New York: Oxford University Press.

Taylor, J., & Cox, B. D. (1997). Microgenetic analysis of group-based solution of complex two-step mathematical word problems by fourth graders. *The Journal of the Learning Sciences, 6*, 183–226.

Valsiner, J. (1987). *Culture and the development of children's action*. New York: Wiley.

Vygotsky, L. (1978). *Mind in society: The development of higher psychological processes*. Cambridge, MA: Harvard University Press.

Vygotsky, L. (1981). The genesis of higher mental functioning. In J. V. Wertsch (Ed.), *The concept of activity in Soviet psychology* (pp. 144–188). Armonk, NY: Sharpe.

Webb, N., & Farivar, S. (1999). Developing productive group interaction in middle school mathematics. In A. O'Donnell & A. King (Eds.), *Cognitive perspectives on peer learning* (pp. 117–150). Mahwah, NJ: Lawrence Erlbaum Associates, Inc.

Webb, N., & Palincsar, A. S. (1996). Group processes in the classroom. In D. Berliner & R. Calfee (Eds.), *Handbook of educational psychology* (pp. 841–876). New York: Macmillan.

Wertsch, J. (1991). *Voices of the mind: A sociocultural approach to mediated action.* Cambridge, MA: Harvard University Press.

Wertsch, J., & Bivens, J. (1992). The social origins of individual mental functioning: Alternatives and perspectives. *Quarterly Newsletter of the Laboratory of Comparative Human Cognition, 14*(2), 35–44.

DISCOURSE PROCESSES, 27(2), 173–185

Typological and Topological Meaning in Diagnostic Discourse

J. L. Lemke
Brooklyn College School of Education
City University of New York

A conceptual distinction between linguistic (and other semiotic) resources for making *typological* (or categorial) versus *topological* (or continuous variation) meanings is used as part of a multimedia semiotic analysis of an episode from a problem-based learning tutorial session in medical education. A semantic analysis of the evaluative language of the participants shows them frequently using various linguistic devices for getting beyond simple "true or false" categorial judgments and also resorting to nonverbal (mainly gestural and graphical) representations when more topological meanings are needed. A tension is identified in medical diagnostic discourse between the typological emphasis of reasoning in terms of diagnostic categories and the frequently topological-quantitative or categorially ambiguous nature of the data and phenomena under discussion.

MULTIDIMENSIONAL MEANING AND VIDEO REALISM

Viewing a 6-min episode from a problem-based learning (PBL) session recorded on videotape, I seem to see and hear several medical students and their "coach" talking, gesturing, looking at and pointing to a complex chart, reading aloud from texts and notes, and generally making meaning by acting in and interacting with one another and the materials around them. I want to briefly analyze a few aspects of their talk and action in order to focus on how and why verbal and visual resources are integrated in this activity and how and why various kinds of evaluative meanings are being made. The analysis is motivated in part by a concern for the materiality of the meaning-making process itself and its implications for the kinds of meanings we make and how we make them. I begin with some reflections on the surprising realism of the video medium, in which the data analyzed here have been recorded, propose an extended semiotic model for mul-

---

Correspondence and requests for reprints should be sent to J. L. Lemke, Brooklyn College School of Education, City University of New York, Brooklyn, NY 11210. E-mail: jllbc@cunyvm.cuny.edu

timedia analysis, and present some highlights from my analysis of the PBL episode.

Videotape and sound-film recording of human social activity are, by the conventions of modernist culture at least, the representational technologies that most closely approximate our "unmediated" social experience. Despite our analytical awareness that camera angles, lighting, and editing techniques must necessarily create artifacts, and that the experience of copresence or interactive participation (even as a silent observer) is fundamentally different from viewing a video, we nevertheless tend to construct a strong sense of "reality" for the world on screen. A transcript of the verbal interactions in a scene is quite lifeless by comparison, even when accompanied by still images that "storyboard" the action. Why does the dynamical integration of speech and image, on a realistic time scale, affect us so strongly? It is not enough to beg the question by constructing similarities to our pervasive life experience, for that still does not tell us what there is about the time-unfolding unities of sight and sound that makes such experiences so much more meaningful to us than texts or still and silent images.

I believe that part of the answer to the mystery of video realism is that we make meaning in social activity in two fundamentally distinct but complementary ways, which I call the *typological* and *topological* modes (discussed later). Moreover, there is clearly something about the dynamical coordination in time (on the millisecond scale) of acoustic and visual input that inclines us to integrate them functionally; that is, we make unified meanings from them, treating them as, in effect, unitary rather than distinct phenomena. This integration is itself achieved through the continuously variable qualities of acoustic–vocal and visual media and, therefore, represents an aspect of their topological meaningfulness.

Typological meaning is the familiar kind described by most theories of linguistics and semiotics: A material form of some sort is assigned to a culturally meaningful category, and the meaning of the category arises from its systematic contrasts with other related categories. In this view of meaning, signs, like words, are assumed to be discrete symbols; as tokens of some type category, they either do or do not possess the various criterial or distinguishing features that define one type as opposed to another. In the neat case of grammatical meaning, a pronoun is either singular or plural; masculine, feminine, or neuter; first, second, or third person. A verb is assigned to just one of a set of possible tenses, and so on. There are no intermediate cases between present and past, declarative and interrogative, singular and plural—or, if there are (as in some languages), they are again represented as additional discrete categories. There is no continuous variation that is meaningful. The continuous variation in the material world is reduced to categorial difference by interpreting a form as an instance of a sign (or at least this is how signs work typologically).

The material forms through which we make typological meaning, however (whether printed word, spoken utterance, or drawn symbol), always also vary from instance to instance in ways that may not be criterial for membership in a sign category but which exhibit continuous variation that is perceivable and to which our cultures do assign meaning. I call meanings made on the basis of continuous or quasi-continuous variation in some property of a material form topological meanings. Really, of course, these are simply two complementary strategies for making meaning, two fundamental modalities of semiosis. The unique acoustic signature of my voice saying a word, compared to other people saying that same word, identifies me to others in a meaningful way based on linguistically noncriterial differences in pronunciation that, in principle, vary continuously. The vocal force or emphasis at a point in my speech and, from one phrase to another, my ability to shift the timbre and sound quality of my voice or prolong particular syllables to create meaningful nuances utilizes the continuous variability of pitch, length, and acoustic harmonics in ways that are counted as *paralinguistic* precisely to the extent that they are not typological. The linguistic system, of course, does allow for some degree of gradations—a case of typology approximating topology—as in evaluative meanings that are inherently gradable semantically across some range from, for example, "totally impossible" through "just barely possible" and "really quite likely" to "absolutely certain." For practical purposes, it is almost always possible to interpolate an intermediate degree of certainty or uncertainty between any two other degrees expressed in words, but the process quickly becomes awkward.

Language, of course, had to evolve to help us make sense of continuous variation in the world in such fundamental matters as spatial and temporal relations and quantity of matter. As we developed technologies and economies in which more and more careful quantitative distinctions were necessary, natural languages became extended semantically by the concepts and symbol systems of mathematics in order to more efficiently represent topological meaning. However, from the earliest recorded times, visual representations were also in use to supplement the limited ability of language to represent spatial relations, such as the angles of a triangle, or quantitative ones, such as nonsimple or even irrational ratios. Visual media such as geometric diagrams or pictures sit still for us, like writing, to allow reinspection and retracing of arguments, and their material extension in space allows iconic representation of continuous variation. Body gestures and communicative movement—visual signs for the observer—also help in the representation of topological meaning.

These two complementary meaning-making strategies always occur together. In speech, word choice and grammatical meaning are essentially typological, intonations and prosodies are both typological and topological, and many voice-quality and quantitative emphasis effects are purely topological. In visual representation, conventional symbols and shapes often make meaning typologically, whereas compositional effects of relative size and placement, or meaningful degrees of variation in hue or saturation of colors, are mainly topological. A gesture may function as a purely typological sign, or it may be articulated dynamically in time to also convey a topological meaning (e.g., degree of impatience). The manual sign languages of the deaf are very similar to speech in combining typologically discrete signs (typically hand shapes) with topologically meaningful modes of articulation of these signs (placement, rates of movement, paths of movement, etc.) in the space between the signers.

Each of these basic modes of meaning making foregrounds particular kinds of potentially meaningful relations and construes *entities*, or units of analysis, as participants in these relations. Most of our conventional representational media (e.g., written text and photographs) either rely far more on one of these two basic semiotic modes than the other or juxtapose the two after having already analytically separated them. They can, at most, offer us their discrete combinatorial possibilities. Video and film media, however, allow us to reconstrue endlessly different intercalibrations of these two kinds of meanings, taking multiple perspectives on how they mutually contextualize one another. Although combinatorial presentations (e.g., texts with images) are discrete and static, even if presented sequentially in time, video and film combine audio and visual information, verbal speech, and visible action dynamically and continuously so that they can be experienced and made sense of simultaneously or sequentially on an unlimited number of timescales.

I am not attempting to argue in this way for any superiority of video or film recordings as scientific data; all records have their special uses. I am trying to foreground the special importance and complexity in video analysis of perspective taking: critically and reflexively making explicit not only the themes and aims of our analyses but the role played by each of the two fundamental semiotic modes, how we are intercalibrating them, and what stance we are taking toward the multiple overlapping timescales dynamically available to our analysis.

In the comments I wish to offer on the 6-min video segment of the interactions among several medical students and their coach, I focus on the relations between these two fundamental modes of meaning construction—the typological and the topological—and on some dynamical phenomena of social activity as a self-organizing process in time.

TYPOLOGICAL AND TOPOLOGICAL MEANING MAKING

The participants in this video episode are engaged in a social activity in which they are constructing an approximation of medical diagnostic discourse. One student in particular (Betty) presents a number of hypotheses about the possible causes of a patient's symptoms, and other students react to these. Their tutor/coach intervenes minimally but attempts to steer the discussion in particular ways.

I want to analyze a tension I perceive in the episode between the norms and strategies of medical diagnostic discourse as practiced by these students, and encouraged by the coach, and the nature of the social–biological phenomena being construed with language and other semiotic resources.

The diagnostic approach, and the underlying medical terminology for events, conditions, and anatomical objects, is fundamentally, in semantic terms, a typological one. That is, it contrasts one diagnostic category with another in either–or terms; it imposes a discrete terminology on continuously varying phenomena and divides even the continuous topography of the brain into bordered territories as seemingly definite as those of nation-states.

Natural phenomena, however, and both natural languages and their technical extensions, also require us to be able to take a more topological approach to making meaning with them. We need to be able to speak of quantitative and continuous variation, of multiple simultaneous and mutually nonexclusive descriptive features, of overlaps and in-betweens, and of matters of degree and instability.

Our dominant intellectual culture, however, privileges the position of classical logic with its narrow view of propositions as eternally either true or false, which in turn requires typological semantic approaches to both reasoning and formal terminological systems. Sharp boundaries are required between this and that, and between true and false, contrary to the bulk of human historical experience, which shows that this is an excessively limiting way to view the world.

Natural language has evolved to provide us with resources for talking about quantity and about degrees of certainty and uncertainty. English and most Indo-European languages, at least, do not basically treat propositions or proposals as either true or false, either good or bad. There are about a half dozen or so semantic properties of propositions, of which *Warrantability*, or relative probability/certainty, is just one among equals (and less frequent and elaborated than, for example, *Desirability*). All of these are very subtly gradable in matters of degree, with a *Polarity* option (binary dichotomy) available in some cases through the grammar (*is* vs. *isn't*) or lexical antonyms such as *true* and *false* or *good* and *bad* (although, semantically, these do not need to be mutually exclusive, except by cultural preference; for this analysis, see Lemke, 1989, 1992, 1998b).

Natural languages have also been extended in those fields (linguistic registers) that have to deal critically with continuous variation and complex quantification. These extensions go, by and large, under the name of *mathematics* insofar as mathematics is simply an extension of the semantics of natural language. The integration of mathematical and verbal reasoning is possible because of this historical relation.

Far older still than mathematics, and also intimately involved in its history, is visual semiotics. We humans make meaning with depictional semiotic resources, ranging from our various conventionalized pictorial resources to more abstract diagrammatic and graphical ones derived from them historically. Writing systems and mathematical symbolisms represent a special case of the general unification of visual and verbal means for making meaningful representations (cf. Cajori, 1928; Harris, 1995; Lemke, 1997). Quantitative reasoning in the sciences represents perhaps the most elaborate case of integrated visual, verbal, and mathematical resources being deployed in meaning making (e.g., see Lemke, 1998a).

Natural language also coevolved with human gestural and postural systems for communications and, indeed, as an integral part of human social activity in all its material, ecological aspects. Ontogenetically, phylogenetically, and historically, speech and gesture share common origins (as do gesture and depiction; see the discussion in Lemke, 1994). Gesture allows us greater latitude and subtlety in making topological meaning relations than do the mainly typological resources of verbal semantics. Spatialization in gesture is akin to spatial representation in depiction.

In the segment transcribed in this special issue, we see two prime instances of the tension between typological-categorial norms in medical diagnostic discourse and the topological-quantitative nature of the biological phenomena being discussed and constructed. One is the imposition of typologically discrete terminology on the quasi-continuous tissue manifold of the human cortex (lines 5–68). The other is the imposition of the typological disjunctions of the mutually exclusive categories of medical diagnosis onto the condition of the patient (see especially lines 155–201). In both cases, some more topological natural language resources, and the topological power of spatializing gestures, are used by the students to help bridge the contradiction and resolve the tension. This is what I want to examine more closely.

THE SETTING AND THE ACTIVITY

The medical school students and their coach are interacting in a PBL session (Koschmann, Myers, Feltovich, & Barrows, 1993–1994). The students are seated around a rectangular table in a small seminar room. From the camera's viewpoint, there is a whiteboard with the patient's case information along the left wall and a very large free-standing chart with sectional views of the human brain behind the opposite end of the table. The principal speaker in the episode is Betty, who sits at the near end (head) of the table, with the coach to her right. Downtable left are Norman and Jenny, at the opposite end (across from Betty) is Lill, and downtable right, beyond the coach, are Maria and May (who does not take a full turn at talk in the episode).

The students are attempting to diagnose the case of a (mainly hypothetical) patient whose presenting symptoms and complete test results are available in a casebook that, in principle, allows fine-grained diagnostic discriminations to be made, but students are expected to access this information only to test specific hypotheses (corresponding to an economical and minimally invasive approach to real patients; cf. the semihumorous remark and responses at lines 257–266).

The transcribed segment begins with Betty's first hypothesis ("my theory," line 1), which leads to a digression on the exact location of the hippocampus in the human brain. We then get a second hypothesis from Betty ("my other theory," line 69) and a debate of the evidence for or against it, which is focused by the coach as an either–or question (line 152). The students find the dichotomy too constraining relative to their interpretation of the case evidence, and this leads them to deploy a number of more topological meaning-making strategies as alternatives to a simple typological diagnosis. No firm conclusion is reached.

Socially, there are at least the following agendas at work:

- The construction, maintenance, and negotiation of group interpersonal relations;
- The negotiated construction of thematic views of medical phenomena; and
- The enactment of cultural and subcultural norms and formations.

These agendas are intimately interwoven and interdependent, as close analysis can show. They include matters of personal dominance and authority, cultural gender roles, the discourse formations of medical theory, and institutional role relationships.

Most of the action in these episodes is talk, and therefore, a linguistic–semantic analysis is most revealing for what meanings are being made through this talk and how. However, there is also significant use of gesture, and in the first episode, use of the visual semiotic resources of the chart is essential. Gestures enable the creation of intermediate alternatives not available in the lexicon of available diagnoses. The chart provides representations of three-dimensional spatial relations within the brain that are not readily described in words. An integrated analysis of at least these three semiotic modalities must be attempted (for prior work on such integration, see Lemke, 1987, 1995a, 1995b, 1998a).

LOCATING THE HIPPOCAMPUS

Let us consider very briefly the first part of the episode, in which, after Betty's suggestion that the lesion causing the symptoms may be near the hippocampus, the coach asks the students: "Where is the hippocampus?" (line 16). What is worth noting here is, first of all, that Betty's immediate reaction is not to begin a verbal answer but to orient to the need for "a picture" (line 17). Verbal language by itself is pretty well powerless to answer the question because its predominantly typological resources may be very good at saying what things are but are rather limited in establishing spatial relations, especially in three dimensions and for spatial regions of irregular shape and not readily visible location.

Norman first points to the chart from his seat; then, he gets up and walks a considerable way to be able to point less ambiguously; and finally, he puts his finger on or almost on the chart (thus minimizing the visual ambiguity due to parallax) and traces the spatial region corresponding to the hippocampus. The information he thus conveys with the help of the chart could not be conveyed verbally in natural language alone.

This procedure is then basically repeated by Lill for a different sectional view of the three-dimensional cortex. Semantic typology is used during the coconstruction of Lill's gestural identification by other participants ("th:at's white matter," line 59; "go to the crevice," line 62; and "that little loop," line 64), but these expressions only work indexically (exophoric spatial deixis) together with the visual–kinesic–spatial resources being deployed here by the group to make meaning topologically. Without the chart being visible to all, these locutions would be functionally useless. At one point, the coach says: "That's it. Tha:t's the hippocampus, then you go over one more gyrus and you're in the temporal lobe" (lines 43–45). His contrastive stress on "temporal" expresses the typological approach of medical scientific terminologies. In fact, no sharp boundaries can be drawn for a "gyrus" or a "lobe." The cortex is a quasi-continuous tissue manifold. Even at the microanatomical level, there would not be such boundaries but rather different cell types intermixing and overlapping in space. I am not even sure if it is absolutely possible to say for any given cell whether it belongs to the hippocampus or not in absolute terms—and it would not necessarily be medically useful to do so.

We see in these portions of the PBL episode examples of the close functional integration of topological and typological strategies and resources for making meaning. They are clearly complementary, but there is also a tension between them produced by the typological bias of medical diagnostic discourse. We also sense here, from the videotape, the dynamics of this functional integration in time (see Hall's, 1999/this issue, account of locating the hippocampus). An even clearer example of dynamic integration occurs in the section of the episode I discuss next; there, the gestural topology helps break down typological diagnostic dichotomies, whereas language is mobilized to express complex degrees of warrantability for various hypoptheses.

BETWEEN TRUE AND FALSE

We turn now to a more central concern of the episode and of medical diagnostic reasoning. It is not just spatial continua that are not well represented by typological semantic strategies, it is also conditions and events. When typological categories are imposed to represent phenomena, propositions made about these phenomena in terms of such categories become problematic. It is not usually possible in life to simply say this is true and that is false, and natural language recognizes this state of affairs semantically by offering us a number of interpolations between polar truth and polar falsity. These have been analyzed in a number of ways in linguistics, most usefully, in my opinion, by Halliday (e.g., Halliday, 1994), whose analysis has been extended in various ways by Martin (1992) and myself

(Lemke, 1998b). My argument here, however, could easily be recast in the terms of other semantic theories.

One interpolation between true and false is that of probability. The Warrantability of a proposition, as a semantic attribute of propositions, is a matter both of degree (how likely) and of polarity (likely to be or likely not to be). We can assert or warrant a proposition both as more or less certain and as more or less uncertain. Another interpolation is that of frequency. The *Usuality* of a proposition is a semantic attribute we can construct for it that tells the speaker's view of how frequent, normal, usual, or expected (or rare, abnormal, unusual, or surprising) it is. A not very well understood, but fairly common, extension of the semantics of Usuality (or perhaps its intersection with the semantics of Temporality) is that of *Stability* or *Temporariness*. What is not usual may also be something newly arisen or something changed from what it has been. It may not be usual because it is only temporarily or recently the case. Finally, it is perhaps worth mentioning that there is a third systematic option in the semantics of evaluating propositions. We may do so with explicit *subjectivity*, saying, for instance, "I am sure that . . ." or "I suspect that . . ." or, we may *objectify* and say, instead, "It is certain that . . ." or "It is possible that . . ."; and, in the extreme polar case, we may simply say, "It is so" or "It is not so."

In lines 136–144, Jenny says that the condition called RIND (reversible ischemic neurological deficit) is "somewhere in be<u>tween</u> a completed stroke and a TIA [transient ischemic attack; another condition]," and she makes a complex gesture coordinating her right hand with "completed stroke" and her left hand with "TIA," creating a gestural space that stands here metaphorically for the topological space of possible meanings in between the typological categories of the diagnosis. Betty then quips, "like . . . unstable angina of the <u>mind</u>" (lines 145–147), making a semantic connection between the issue of Stability or Temporariness and the continuum of possible conditions under discussion.

These conditions differ from each other, so far as is said here, in part by a quantitative difference in how long symptoms persist. That quantitative difference can be represented spatially in contrast with the discreteness of the typological diagnostic categories, and the instability of the symptoms or condition contrasts with the implicit stability of the notion that a patient "has a condition." The students laugh here over the tension between a norm of clear-cut, right-or-wrong diagnosis, with its scientific definitiveness, and the fuzzy nature of the phenomena they must deal with.

When Jenny coarticulates her gestures and speech (including the vocal gesture of the pitch pattern for "in be<u>tween</u>," line 142), there is again a dynamic integration in time that has special force in the video but is lost in the transcript, even if supplemented by a still photo or photo sequence, of her gesture. What linguistics and kinesics separate for analytical purposes, the physiology and functionality of human communication fuse as a unitary perceptual phenomenon and meaning reality. No doubt, they are fused as well for Jenny in the process of producing coordinated voicing and moving, and insofar as we as viewers, or Jenny's coparticipants face-to-face, are entrained by the *interactional synchronies* (Condon & Ogston, 1967; Kendon, 1973) of the dynamic situation, they are fused for us as well. A focus on topological strategies and resources for making meaning cannot be separated from a concern for the general materiality, including bodily involvement, of sense making. This applies both to the primary participants in the video and to ourselves as secondary participants interacting with the video.

Returning to the analysis proper, we find the coach a moment later again pressing a typological view: "So which one did he ha:ve?" (line 152). The responses begin with Maria's "he's (.) progressing to a stroke" (lines 155, 157), which emphasizes instability through the aspectual semantics of verbs (the ways we express incipience, progression, habituality, completion, etc., of processes). Norman comments, "A little bit of both" (line 156), thus implicitly challenging the either–or semantics of typological categories and the coach's "which one?" Betty then begins (line 158) another long discussion that turns on the stability of the patient's condition and symptoms.

In the course of this activity (see lines 202–204), Norman rather forcefully frames the instability with a contrast between "we're seeing an- an acute leg deficit" and "now (.) we're seeing five over five strength," and he makes hand gesture movements to accentuate this instability and temporariness. (Note that the issue of temporariness and change had been introduced initially by the coach in line 104: "So why do the leg findings go away?") Typological categories stand synoptically outside of time in an eternal Platonic present of abstract relations. Even continuous change in properties can be assimilated to this paradigm (one of the triumphs of modern mathematics and science), but what about intermittent, discontinuous, unreliable, unstable, and merely temporary phenomena or symptoms? Part of video realism, as of life, is the meaningfulness of such phenomena. In language, they are not readily represented in individual clauses but can be approximated over the course of longer texts or narratives. In visual semiotics, again, we require a dimension of time (in production, presentation, or interpretation) to represent them.

The PBL discussion next moves on to the other main symptom, a problem with verbal language. In lines 214–219, Norman argues that the patient's speech is "screwed up," and Betty challenges this in a polar and typological way: "Is it screwed up?" Norman asserts again with a qualification—"somehow"—which is a shade less definitive than the pure polar choice. Betty concedes only in topological terms—"a little bit"—and makes a gesture with her fingers held extremely close together. *It is* versus *it isn't* has been converted again to a matter of in between, of degree, of manner, and of how much. This is not the end of the discussion: In her follow-up (lines 226–232), Betty invokes a whole host of Usuality resources (*occasionally, rarely,* and *often*) and a construction of Instability (one part of the mental status exam vs. "the rest" of it).

By the time Betty gets to her conclusion (lines 234–239), the resources of Warrant-by-degree are in full sway: "I don't kno:w" (i.e., no polar assertion and no high degree of warrantability), "I think," "would prob'ly lean more towards" (lower degrees of probability and warrant), together with the associated Instability, "something transient that comes'n goes" and "at a fairly good moment."

Her final argument again turns on Instability (lines 245–251), that things must have been worse at one time than they are "right now." Again, her hands seem to move to show the temporal dynamics she is trying to construct, as opposed to a more static or synoptic view of a patient's definitive condition.

CONCLUSIONS

My point here is not that medical diagnostic discourse is inappropriate to the real complexity of biological and social phenomena but that a formal emphasis on typological meaning constructions, on definitive categorizations and sharp boundaries, is necessarily in tension with the topological aspects of the phenomena. Natural language gives us some topological resources for making the kinds of meaning that are needed in such situations, and together with gestural and visual semiotic resources, as extended by mathematics and quantitative reasoning, we are reasonably well positioned to deal with them. In this episode, when the tension is strongest, the students bring these resources to bear. Both topological and typological meaning-making strategies are necessary; purely classificatory reasoning, pure classical *reductio* and *excluded-middle* reasoning is not sufficient.

The coach here has mainly been pressing for a typological approach, and perhaps that is, at times, a valuable heuristic, forcing the sort of appeal to counterevidence that also occurs in the episode. His summary comment, "Some patients are vague . . . don't give you the answers you wanna hear" (lines 262–266), can, however, be taken as marginalizing this particular case rather than emphasizing how typical it is that instances do not quite fit general categories, putting the blame on the patient, or ratifying that the students should "wanna hear" more definitive answers. I am not blaming the coach, and I may not be interpreting him generously enough. Perhaps in other episodes with this group there is more emphasis on quantitative metrics and on the impossibility of making exact mappings between continuously varying phenomena and discrete diagnostic categories. The resources the students bring to play, both semantic and gestural, seem to stand outside the official norms of the discourse, and yet they are clearly critical to making the meanings that need to be made here.

There is a great need in scientific education, especially when dealing with complex and individualized systems (e.g., local and planetary meteorology, organisms, ecosystems, etc.) to better understand the role of topological meaning in verbal semantics and reasoning, in gestural–kinesic and visual semiotics, and in the integration of mathematics with both verbal and visual reasoning. I believe that a semiotic analysis of the kind I have tried to sketch here offers some useful tools for doing this.

Regarding the video-recording medium itself, I think the points made here should be sufficient to suggest that the dynamic integration of gestural and visual communication with speech is often essential to characterizations of the kinds of meanings participants make in an interaction. It is not simply that the significance of a gesture becomes more focal when we see it coproduced with, for example, speech that is constructing degrees of warrant or usuality, but that the foregrounding of such gradable meanings in the event is itself coproduced, for the participants as well as for us, by such phenomena. Meanings of many different kinds inevitably get produced in most interactions, but some kinds become more salient than others for participants, and that salience, in turn, sets the stage for what is more likely to emerge next in an interaction. Although we may segment activity into this or that unit of action according to a particular focus of interest, and criteria based on the occurrence of verbal, gestural, or other signs relevant to that interest, video analysis still shows us that activity is continuous and that every action or sign may be construed as belonging to ongoing processes on multiple timescales and, therefore, subserving multiple social functions. We cannot account for the dynamical, self-organizing, and emergent character of spontaneous social interaction and activity if our data, or our focus on the data, artificially dismembers the unity of meaningful action into what our various semiotic analyses (linguistic, kinesic, graphical, etc.) have evolved to describe separately. If we separate, it should only be in order to more richly reconnect.

REFERENCES

Cajori, F. (1928). *A history of mathematical notations.* Chicago: Open Court Publishing.

Condon, W. S., & Ogston, W. D. (1967). A segmentation of behavior. *Journal of Psychiatric Research, 5,* 221–235.

Hall, R. (1999/this issue). The organization and development of discursive practices for "having a theory." *Discourse Processes, 27,* 187–218.

Halliday, M. A. K. (1994). *An introduction to functional grammar* (2nd ed.). London: Edward Arnold.

Harris, R. (1995). *Signs of writing.* London: Routledge.

Kendon, A. (1973). The role of visible behavior in the organization of social interaction. In M. von Cranach & I. Vine (Eds.), *Social communication and movement* (pp. 29–74). New York: Academic.

Koschmann, T. D., Myers, A. C., Feltovich, P. J., & Barrows, H. S. (1993–1994). Using technology to assist in realizing effective learning and instruction: A principled approach to the use of computers in collaborative learning. *The Journal of the Learning Sciences, 3,* 227–264.

Lemke, J. L. (1987). Strategic deployment of speech and action: A sociosemiotic analysis. In J. Evans & J. Deely (Eds.), *Semiotics 1983: Proceedings of the Semiotic Society of America "Snowbird" Conference* (pp. 67–79). New York: University Press of America.

Lemke, J. L. (1989). Semantics and social values. *Word, 40*(1–2), 37–50.

Lemke, J. L. (1992). Interpersonal meaning in discourse: Value orientations. In M. Davies & L. Ravelli (Eds.), *Advances in systemic linguistics: Recent theory and practice* (pp. 82–104). London: Pinter.

Lemke, J. L. (1994, December). *Multiplying meaning: Literacy in a multimedia world.* Paper presented at the National Reading Conference, Charleston SC. (ERIC Document Reproduction Service No. ED 365 940)

Lemke, J. L. (1995a, April). *Emergent agendas in collaborative activity.* Paper presented at the annual meeting of the American Educational Research Association, San Francisco. (ERIC Document Reproduction Service No. ED 386 425)

Lemke, J. L. (1995b, April). *Making towers, making withs.* Paper presented at the meeting of the National Association for Research in Science Teaching, San Francisco. (ERIC Document Reproduction Service No. ED 384 513)

Lemke, J. L. (1997). Review of *Signs of writing* (Roy Harris). *Functions of Language, 4*(1), 125–129.

Lemke, J. L. (1998a). Multiplying meaning: Visual and verbal semiotics in scientific text. In J. R. Martin & R. Veel (Eds.), *Reading science* (pp. 87–113). London: Routledge.

Lemke, J. L. (1998b). Resources for attitudinal meaning: Evaluative orientations in text semantics. *Functions of Language, 5*(1), 33–56.

Martin, J. R. (1992). *English text.* Philadelphia: Benjamins.

DISCOURSE PROCESSES, 27(2), 187–218
Copyright © 1999, Lawrence Erlbaum Associates, Inc.

The Organization and Development of Discursive Practices for "Having a Theory"

Rogers Hall

Graduate School of Education
University of California, Berkeley

This article compares cases of "having a theory" from two settings: a fragment of problem-based instruction recorded in a medical school (the recording analyzed in this special issue) and a published analysis of dinner table stories told among 5-year-old children, their older siblings, and parents (Ochs, Taylor, Rudolph, & Smith, 1992). In each setting, people propose what they or we might call "theories"; then, these proposals are questioned, elaborated, and evaluated in conversation. Two questions drive this comparative analysis: (a) How do people make and use representations to bring theoretical entities, processes, and evaluations into conversation? and (b) How can an analysis of discursive practices across settings be specific about possible developmental trajectories? These questions lead to a potential paradox for studies of talk in interaction. On one hand, we render the practices of professional "technoscientists" as being ordinary; on the other hand, we render the practices of people in "ordinary conversation" as being scientific. Either this is a crisis for comparative research on the discursive practices of technoscience, or we face an opportunity to rebalance studies of the organization and development of discipline-specific competencies.

My analysis of the fragment of conversation at the center of this special issue focuses on two questions: (a) How are a missing patient, his complaints, his particular brain, and "The Brain" brought together in conversation as people are "having a theory"? and (b) What can comparative analysis tell us about the development of discipline-specific representational practices across settings in which people are said to be having a theory? I use "The Brain" to describe an authoritative technical object (i.e., a generic or idealized human brain) that is a resource for participants throughout this fragment of conversation. I quote "having a theory" to foreground the activities of theorizing or "theory sequences," as they

Correspondence and requests for reprints should be sent to Rogers Hall, Graduate School of Education, University of California, Berkeley, CA 94720. E-mail: rhall@socrates.berkeley.edu

are described in a published analysis of this fragment of conversation (Glenn, Koschmann, & Conlee, 1995). Similarly, I follow Ochs, Taylor, Rudolph, and Smith (1992) in describing dinner time conversations as a "theory-building activity." The purposes and methods of these two studies differ, but both foreground the work of having a theory as a particular form of discursive practice.

In this article, I first describe why these questions are important and list several limitations on secondary analysis of fragments of conversation as an empirical basis for studying having a theory. Caveats in place, I then explore each question with an analysis of how theories are achieved in conversation, ranging across conversations in medical school and at the family dinner table. Finding ample evidence of similarity in the way that medical students and family members go about having a theory, I then consider a potential paradox for comparative studies of talk in interaction. The paradox arises when activities of technoscience and ordinary conversation are rendered in ways that make them indistinguishable without extrinsic (i.e., outside the analysis) reference to who people are or to the settings in which they participate. Depending on how we approach the production (or reproduction) of disciplinary knowledge, this could either be a crisis for comparative research on the discursive practices of technoscience or a long-overdue reframing for studies of discipline-specific competencies and their development.

GETTING BRAINS INTO CONVERSATION

My approach to exploring how materials are brought together when having a theory will be both prospective (i.e., what actually happens in ongoing interaction?) and retrospective (i.e., how is it that material resources take the shape that they do?). The retrospective line of analysis follows what Akrich (1992) and Latour (1987, 1992) called restoring the "missing masses" in technoscience. Their project is to invent a sociology that can include both humans and technoscientific objects, an approach to understanding human activity that neither (a) ignores its material infrastructure nor (b) assumes that this infrastructure completely determines action. For example, as Latour (1996a) struggled to render the complex, sociotechnical trajectory of a rapid-transit system, he framed the sociological problem in this way:

> [Sociologists] need to have infinite respect for the deciphering of inscriptions. To propose the description of a technological mechanism is to extract from it precisely the script that the engineers had transcribed in the mechanisms and the automatisms of humans or nonhumans. It is to retrace the path of incarnation in the other direction. It is to rewrite in words and arguments what has become, what might have become, thanks to the intermediary of mechanisms, a mute function. (p. 207)

Latour's (1996b) solution to the problem of understanding material infrastructure is to operate the machinery of sociology both forward in time, watching people inscribe social relations into technical objects, and backward in time, de-(in)scribing the missing masses who have done the work of inscription and so live on in the potential of the objects that surround us.

Approached in this way, exploring how materials are brought together when having a theory in medical school will require that we (a) open up some of the texts these students and their "coach" are using and (b) ask how they manage to animate (make present or re-present) the variety of people and things that are absent when their conversation begins. Not only do we need to restore these missing masses in an analysis of doing, teaching, and learning technoscientific work (in this case, differential diagnosis in a clinical setting) but the students and their coach apparently need to do this work themselves. In this sense, having a theory about trouble in the brain requires mobilizing a substantial history of technoscientific work, and this may need to happen each and every time the theory is "had."

FOLLOWING DEVELOPMENTAL TRAJECTORIES
FOR HAVING A THEORY

The second question I focus on in this analysis concerns where we expect to find people having a theory and how these settings could be linked together through a plausible developmental trajectory. I approach this question in a comparative fashion, drawing on what Ochs et al. (1992) called an "opportunity space" for building theories, something they found and studied in the context of dinner table conversations:

> Collaborative storytelling is a vehicle by which families—in varying degrees and styles—socialize their children into certain linguistic, social, and cognitive structures and practices that constitute "scientific" discourse and thought, potentially long before they enter kindergarten. Our data show that at dinnertime . . . children are audience to and often direct contributors to jointly produced narratives in which co-narrators construct and evaluate explanations of events and thus engage in basic processes of scientific thought. (p. 40)

The puzzle about development is how we should think about lining up 5-year-olds at the dinner table with these medical students, when all are said to be doing the work of having a theory. We could also look for having a theory in other types of activity (Levinson, 1992). These might include (a) hypothetical narratives used to organize practice sessions in Little League baseball (Heath, 1991), (b) talk between mothers and small children as they measure ingredients and follow recipes in kitchens (Callanan, Shrager, & Moore, 1995), (c) discussions among middle school science students designing representations of motion (diSessa, Hammer, Sherin, & Kolpakowski, 1991), (d) talk about graphical representations during meetings between empirical and theoretical physicists (Ochs, Jacoby, & Gonzales, 1994), (e) hierarchically organized laboratory practices of neuroendocrinologists (Latour & Woolgar, 1979), (f) the coordinated use of data-gathering devices across different disciplines on a research ship (C. Goodwin, 1995), or (g) the construction of competing historical narratives about the Great Plains as an ecosystem during the 1930s (Cronon, 1992).

If having a theory is an activity system that is important for family, school, and workplace discourse, then how do people find trajectories into these practices and how could we distinguish one form of participation from another? In exploring this question, I borrow and slightly rework Schegloff's (1992) principle of "procedural consequentiality" recommended for studies of talk in interaction:

> How does the fact that the talk is being conducted in some setting (e.g., "the hospital") issue in any consequence for the shape, form, trajectory, content, or character of the interaction that the parties conduct? And what is the mechanism by which the context-so-understood has determinate consequences for the talk? (p. 111)

Holding an analysis of human activity accountable to the methods by which participants in that activity conduct and make sense of their interaction is a foundational concern for research in ethnomethodology and conversation analysis (see Glenn, Koschmann, & Conlee, 1999/this issue), particularly as these traditions attempt to "respecify" theoretical constructs for understanding language, cognition, work, and society. For example, Lynch (1991) examined specific measurement practices in sociology, household kitchens, everyday conversations about timing or scheduling, legal testimony, and a research laboratory in the neurosciences. He argued that there is no pregiven method for mathematizing experience across these diverse settings and that, instead, we should investigate how "measures" or "precision" are organized and made relevant in each.

In studies of learning and teaching, it may be helpful to pursue a notion of consequentiality that looks at both the organization and development of technoscientific practices. That is, we should ask how it is that participants in conversations like this problem-based learning (PBL) episode (i.e., the fragment analyzed in this special issue) demonstrate to themselves and others that the current conduct of activity is moving along some developmental trajectory (i.e., someone is learning to participate in the activity system or the system itself is being reorganized with respect to some purpose). This preserves a focus on how analytic categories become relevant and are actually achieved in interaction while directing the analysis toward events that make up activities called *learning* and *teaching*. Therefore, within this article, I attempt to focus on the "developmental consequentiality" of an activity system that I call "having a theory."

LIMITATIONS ON SECONDARY ANALYSIS
OF CONVERSATIONAL FRAGMENTS

In my view, there are serious limitations on using fragments of conversation as the basis for posing and investigating these types of questions. First, analyzing interaction without understanding the context for that interaction risks misinter-pretation (Cicourel, 1992; Jordan & Henderson, 1995), even if we assume that participants in some fragment are exhibiting the methods by which they manage to carry off the activity. My analysis, along with all the others in this special issue, runs this risk.

Second, many of the phenomena I would like to follow in this fragment fall outside the frame of video and audio records made of the conversation. For example, using a single camera, it is difficult to follow how participants orient to each other and to the variety of inscribed forms that are distributed around the room. The details of these forms and their active use are only partly available for analysis, so I will look closely at phenomena I can recover and bracket my analysis accordingly. Records of human activity are always selective (Hall, in press-b), and the close analysis of naturally occurring representational practices makes heavy demands on existing techniques for recording (C. Goodwin, 1981, pp. 37–46, 1993b; Hutchins, 1995a, pp. 21–26).

Finally, I do not study instructional practices in medicine, so I have limited familiarity with both the content and the organization of these kinds of conver-sations. Problem- or case-based instruction is intended to simulate "authentic" aspects of medical practice (Barrows, 1994; Williams, 1992), so I assume that this PBL fragment sits somewhere between what Atkinson and Delamont (1977) called "hot" and "cold" medicine. In their analysis of more traditional medical instruction, cold medicine consisted of patient encounters that were staged by teaching faculty for medical school residents, and under these circumstances (i.e., teaching rounds), "live" patients had to be carefully managed to present well-structured diagnostic problems for students. In contrast, hot medicine consisted of shift duty in an emergency clinic on weekends, a time when senior medical staff were generally unavailable. In this situation, medical students were expected to act as doctors in unscripted and sometimes life-threatening situations.

Although I think the novelty of this PBL conversation is both a strength and a weakness of the articles assembled in this issue, my analyses does not attempt to render this material as exemplary in some broader educational enterprise. Caveats in place, I now turn to an analysis of the two questions leading this article.

FINDING TROUBLE IN THE BRAIN

Question 1: How are a missing patient, his complaints, his particular brain, and "The Brain" brought together in conversation as people are "having a theory"?

In beginning an analysis, we face the immediate problem that the "start" of this fragment occurs within an ongoing conversation, coinciding with the coach's summary that "we're pretty confident"[1] the patient's trouble is located on the left side of the brain. In the introduction to this special issue, Koschmann tells us where the students and the coach are sitting, but where are the patient, his brain, his wife, the medical history giving his "problem," or the person taking that history?

As the video camera pans around the room to follow the speakers, we see a whiteboard covered with writing, a table surface informally partitioned into local workspaces (i.e., individual piles of textbooks, notes, and other bound documents), and a neuroanatomical flip chart showing a three-by-three array of brain sections. Students write notes on the whiteboard to record the medical history and laboratory tests of an elderly man, fictitiously named Jake Elwood. His difficulties are the subject of a carefully crafted teaching case (i.e., what Betty calls "the book," line 258), and other texts on the table include a pathology textbook called "Harrison's" (used in Betty's initial theory and mentioned explicitly by Jenny, line 130). The flip chart is a prominent technical display, consisting of a heterogeneous collection of technical images for locating structures in the human brain (see Figure 1). For example, the center image shows the brain surrounded by a human head with skull and neck vertebra; other images show a naked brain (i.e., no surrounding head), either as two-dimensional sections or as three-dimensional brains that are partially dissected, using cutaway views to reveal internal structures. This is a dense ecology of representational forms (Hall, in press-a; Star, 1995), but nowhere can we see an elderly man complaining of difficulty in speaking, poor memory, or weak legs. His brain, presumably the source of his troubles, is nowhere at hand, and we do not find his concerned wife or the physician (or nurse) who took his medical history and gave him a "mental status exam" (lines 175–176).

How can we start with so many things missing? These are not just our problems, of course: How can these students and their coach keep the conversation going? Students in this PBL meeting face these sense-making difficulties, and I assume that similar difficulties would be found in any context in which medical decision making proceeds on the basis of incomplete clinical records that include subjective (i.e., patient-generated) and objective (i.e., specialist-generated) findings. For example, Musen, Wieckert, Miller, Campbell, and Fagan (1995) described how tensions between subjective and objective findings surface during the development of an electronic patient-record system. These kinds of systems may become stable, even standardized technical objects in clinical medicine (Berg, 1997), similar to the reference texts and flip chart present in this PBL meeting.

---

[1]In the PBL transcript originally provided for my analysis, several additional turns at talk were included at the beginning and at the end of the transcript published in this special issue. The coach's summary comes from these earlier utterances. Unless otherwise noted, line numbers in this article match those listed in the transcript for this special issue.

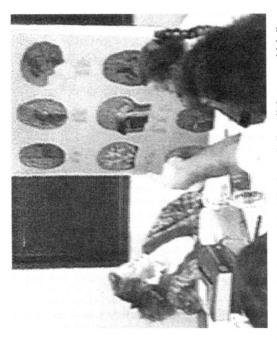

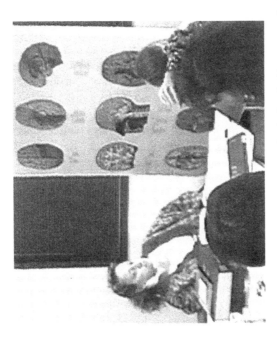

FIGURE 1 Two coordinated assemblies for finding the hippocampus. In the left frame, Maria (bottom right) lifts the occluding "little temporal lobe" to reveal the hippocampus as Lill (top left) looks on (lines 29–30); in the right frame, the coach (bottom left) directs students to "point to it" in a flip chart rendering The Brain (line 32).

Clearly, some of this sense-making work has already been established as the fragment begins, but this work is ongoing. I want to look carefully at how all these absences are made present as the conversation proceeds.

Having a Theory About a Vascular Lesion

Betty (or perhaps Koschmann's selection presented in the introduction to the special issue) wastes no time in getting a theory into the conversation. From lines 1 to 14, Betty sets out her first theory: The patient's difficulties are caused by a vascular lesion, originating in anterior cerebral circulation and affecting sensory and motor pathways in the hippocampus. After the coach initiates an extended effort to locate the generic hippocampus (lines 16–68), Betty presents her second theory (lines 69–122): The patient has a space-occupying lesion in the "posterior limb of the internal capsule"[2] that is pressing on spinal nerves and interfering with his motor function. In terms of propositional content, both of Betty's theories turn on the location of a lesion or tumor in this patient's (still missing) brain. Not surprisingly, much of this multiparty talk requires that participants jointly find their way around in a three-dimensional object that is not visually or manually available. I look closely at Betty's first theory here, then turn to collective efforts to find the hippocampus in the next section.

Betty starts her first theory about a vascular lesion by speaking for herself, the medical text in front of her, and Maria (e.g., "what *it* [italics added] said in here, n-*my* [italics added] theory," line 1; gaze is fully on Text). She then speaks more exclusively for herself, comparing two locations in the brain (i.e., "*I think* [italics added] the hippocampus is like a lot more medial," lines 11–12; gaze directed to the coach). Her spatial comparison contrasts different causes for the lesion, one "deep in the temporal lobe" (lines 5–6, also attributed to Maria) and the other stemming from "anterior cerebral circulation" (line 14). The anterior location and cause (a vascular lesion) is the gist of Betty's first theory, apparently intended for the coach as a primary recipient.

Three phenomena are relevant to understanding how people and brains get organized for having a theory during Betty's extended turn at talk. First, the theory is authored by multiple agents, brought together in the voice of a single speaker. Rather than presenting her theory alone, Betty enlists the text and Maria as partial allies before presenting her own ideas (i.e., what "I think," lines 11–14). Second, the theory rests implicitly on the organization of The Brain and its mapping onto the particular brain of a patient. To do this, the grouping of Betty/Text/Maria shift from the coach's prior talk about a particular patient's brain into a discussion of the location of generic brain structures. Third, the

---

[2]I am at the limit of my familiarity with brain structure in using these terms. Koschmann (personal communication, November 3, 1997) tells me that the hippocampus and the internal capsule are close together, but they are different brain structures.

articulated assembly of a patient's brain, a clinical syndrome (i.e., "amnesic dysnomic aphasia," line 4), and generic brain structures involves considerable uncertainty. This uncertainty is expressed both by the text (i.e., the cause is "usually" deep and "presumably" interrupts connections, lines 5, 7) and in the way that Betty hedges when delivering her theory (i.e., "I think," line 11, and "might be," line 13). Therefore, having a theory, at least in this instance, involves multiple authors, implicit but complex forms of generalization, and marked efforts to identify and to manage uncertainty.

Pursuing the Hippocampus Across Representational Media

Because Betty's first theory depends heavily on the location of the hippocampus in relation to other structures in The Brain, its precise location should be highly relevant. The coach apparently agrees because he changes the topic and emphasizes its uncertain location when he asks, "Where is the [italics added] hippocampus" (line 16). What results looks like an instructional sequence in neuroanatomy: Betty's extended turn comes to an end, there is a pronounced shift in orientation among her student peers, and they jointly undertake an episode of collective wayfinding in The Brain. This wayfinding episode, which ends with a stable location for the hippocampus, gets all of the following contributions into coordination:

- Betty's appeal to a "picture" of the generic brain (line 17);
- Norman's spoken and physical selection of one graphical plate from the flip chart (lines 19–22);
- Maria's spoken and then gesturally enacted attempt to move deeper into the generic brain (lines 24, 27, 29–31);
- Jenny's temporary loss of memory (line 25);
- The coach's directions to look at a different graphical plate (a "section") on the flip chart (lines 28, 32, 33);
- The coach's attempt to locate the hippocampus in relation to the temporal lobe (i.e., "you go over one more gyrus," lines 43–45);
- The coach's directions to find the hippocampus in another graphical section (i.e., "see it on the frontal," lines 47–48);
- Lill's selection of a region that the coach subsequently disqualifies as "white matter" (line 57); and
- Maria and Norman's jointly produced identification of a "crevice" containing the relevant structure (i.e., "That little loop," lines 61–66).

Things are coming together, but how? The patient, having contributed his specific difficulties (e.g., a numb leg), has dropped out of the interaction in favor of structures within The Brain. The problem for analysis, then, is to follow how Betty's contrast ("deep" vs. "a lot more medial," lines 5, 12) is somehow transformed into a stable, authoritative location in this generic brain. As the previous list indicates, finding the hippocampus during this episode is a widely distributed, collective achievement. The distributions run across people and their relations of accountability, across ordinary and technical language terms, across different modes of activity, and across different representational media. I consider each briefly.

Distributions across people and relations of accountability. Different people make contributions during this wayfinding episode. Table 1, read from top to bottom, shows that these contributions produce at least four distinctly different representations of location, with Locations 4 and 5 (lines 57 and 61) providing intermediate stops on the way to selecting Location 6 in a frontal view of The Brain. Within this episode, there is a significant disagreement about where the hippocampus is actually located. The disagreement is over Norman's initial selection of Location 1 in the flip chart (lines 19–22), which Maria disputes with a gestural depiction of Location 2 (i.e., a location "un:der that," lines 24, 27–31). After mapping Maria's contribution onto a more conventional view in the flip chart (Location 3), the coach juxtaposes the temporal lobe with the hippocampus in this same graphical image (lines 43–46). He then directs students to find the hippocampus in a different conventional view of The Brain (i.e., to "see it on the frontal" view, lines 47–48). When the coach closes this anatomy lesson ("That's it," line 68), he and the students appear to agree about the location of the hippocampus (Location 6). We cannot be sure what different participants understand at this point, but various disagreements pursued during the wayfinding episode end as topics in the conversation (e.g., between Norman and Maria, lines 22–24, 26–27), and Betty takes this closing as a relevant moment to present her second theory (i.e., "My other theory," line 69). Moreover, she uses the settled position of the hippocampus as a background resource for her second theory (i.e., "if it was right there ((*points to chart*))," lines 71–72).

The distribution of wayfinding across relations of accountability is more difficult to follow, but two features of this episode are important to notice. First, the coach acts and is received as a teacher who directs the efforts of students (i.e., an institutionally sanctioned authority). His requests for precise locations in the flip chart are met with collective activity by students, and his assessments of these activities either lead to closings (e.g., positive assessments at lines 43 or 68) or to alternative courses of action (e.g., negative assessments at lines 50–51 or 59–60). The second feature to notice, however, is that the coach is not the only relevant authority in this conversation. Betty is able to resume her extended turn at theorizing, taking the collective answer to this wayfinding episode as material for her second run at having a theory (i.e., she acts and is received as the author of these theories). Her second theory is challenged by her peers and the coach (e.g., lines 79–85), but it is her theory, and she is given ample interactional space to present and defend it.

TABLE 1

Contributions by Different Speakers While Finding the Hippocampus

Selected Location of the Hippocampus	Line Numbers	Primary Speaker(s)	Contribution to the Wayfinding Episode
Location 1: "((Walks over to chart, points)) Right in here"	19–22	Norman	Norman moves to the top right image of the flip chart and locates what others see as the temporal lobe
Location 2: "Sts-lk-if you lift (("lifting" gesture with right arm, elbow out)) up that little temporal lobe, it's on the inside"	27, 29–31	Maria	Maria's gesture animates and reveals an alternative location, "un:der" the temporal lobe
Location 3: "You can point to it on the middle top"	28, 32–43	Coach, Maria, and Lill	The coach maps Maria's embodied alternative onto the "middle top" image in the flip chart
Location 3/Location 1: "tha:t's the hippocampus, then you go over one more gyrus and you're in the temporal lobe"	43–46	Coach and Maria	The coach colocates the hippocampus (Maria's alternative) and the temporal lobe (Norman's initial selection) in the same conventional view of The Brain (i.e., "middle top")
Location 6: "That's it"	47–68	Coach, Lill, Maria, and Norman	The coach directs students to find the hippocampus in a different conventional view of The Brain (i.e., "on the frontal")

Note. Norman's initial selection (Location 1) is disputed by Maria (Location 2); the coach then maps Maria's gestured alternative onto the flip chart (Location 3); the coach then colocates both alternatives in the chart (Location 3/Location 1) and asks students to find the hippocampus in a different conventional view of The Brain (i.e., "see it on the frontal").

Distributions across ordinary and technical language. The work of having a theory is also distributed across different types of language for describing
spatial locations (for a comparison of typological and topological resources in
language, see Lemke, 1999/this issue). Some of these oppositional terms are
common in everyday usage (e.g., "up" and "down" or "here" and "there"),
whereas others either index graphical sections of The Brain by their position in
the flip chart (e.g., "middle top" and "second row left") or by standard orthographic perspective (e.g., "medial" [?lateral] and "frontal" [?occipital]). In listing
these oppositions, I need to guess at unspoken terms, so I precede these with a
question mark and quote the terms that are actually spoken (e.g., "medial" [?lat-
eral]). When used in a coordinated fashion, these terms allow the students and
the coach to find different structural locations in The Brain.

Movement between ordinary and technical language provides further support
for viewing this wayfinding episode as an anatomy lesson. Of course, there is
nothing essentially technical about terms like "middle" or "top" (e.g., the coach's
directions, line 28). However, in concert with a representational technology like
the neuroanatomical flip chart, these terms do increase the degree of specification
available to participants in the conversation (i.e., they allow participants to con-
verge on a precise location within The Brain).

Across the episode, the coach edits student contributions to arrive at a spatial
representation of the hippocampus using a conventional technical reading of the
flip chart. For example, Betty initially orients to "a picture *up there*" [italics
added] (line 17), then Norman interrupts her to select a location that is "*down
there* [italics added]," at the "*bottom of this* thing [italics added]," and "right *in
here* [italics added]" (lines 19–22). Even as Maria disagrees with Norman, the
coach begins asking for a location "on the middle, *middle top* [italics added]"
of the flip chart (line 28). He then maps Maria's gestural representation revealing
the hippocampus onto this same graphical image (lines 32–33). As the episode
draws to a close, he compares the locations of the temporal lobe and hippocampus
within this image and asks for identification of the hippocampus "on the *frontal*
[italics added]" image in the flip chart (lines 47–48).

Distributions across modes of activity. Maria's sustained disagreement
with Norman's initial location in the flip chart is particularly interesting, both as
a coordinated use of talk and gesture and in its relation to the flip chart as a
visually prominent, technical inscription. Maria's gesture (lines 24–31) looks like
a form of manual dissection and consists of four major parts: (a) Her right hand
comes to the center of the gestural stage and appears to hook something on
"sts-lk-if you"; (b) she lifts her right arm and her hand, still holding a hooked
position, as she says "lift"; (c) she holds her right hand at her forehead on "little
temporal lobe" (see Figure 1); and finally (d) she returns her right hand to the
center position while saying "on the inside." Interpreted as a series of iconic displays
in gestural space (McNeill, 1992, pp. 86–91), Maria lifts an occluding temporal
lobe out of the way to reveal the hippocampus, nestled in the space underneath.

As shown in the image on the left in Figure 1, her gaze is directed across the table and away from the flip chart, so it is likely that she is narrating and showing the perspective of someone doing this kind of anatomical procedure (i.e., the referent of "you" includes herself and recipients of her talk). In concert, Lill turns away from the flip chart when Maria begins, watches as the occluding structure is lifted away in Maria's gestural stage (left image in Figure 1), then turns back to the flip chart after Maria shows the location of the previously hidden hippocampus. The image to the right in Figure 1 (line 32) shows the coach's attempt to map Maria's contribution onto the flip chart by directing students to "point to it on the middle top."

Coordinating talk and action with inscription.   The distribution of wayfinding across different modes of action (pointing, physical orientation, and manual or gestural dissection) serves to coordinate talk with more durable, inscribed representational forms. As the episode proceeds, there are several shifts in representational media that are critical to producing a settled location for the hippocampus: (a) from ordinary to technical language, (b) from talk to action (e.g., bodily orientation, gaze, and gesture) to conventional representational views of The Brain, and (c) from a single location for this structure to an articulated set of orthogonal views. Respectively, these shifts support more precise spatial description, a mapping of utterances onto more durable representational technologies (i.e., images in the flip chart), and a relational comparison of different spatial locations for a single brain structure (i.e., Norman's vs. Maria's locations for the hippocampus).

By following distributions across multiple speakers, language terms, action, and inscribed forms separately, we make visible some of the complexity of this wayfinding episode. Only when these distributed resources are brought into coordination is it possible for participants to line up subjective and objective findings, particular and generic brains, causes and effects, and competing theories. The collective, interactional details of finding the hippocampus during this wayfinding episode are a critical part of this larger sense-making enterprise.

Present- and Past-Time Resources for Managing Uncertainty

As I argued earlier, mapping particular instances onto multiple, possibly overlapping generalizations requires that people manage uncertainty. Has this patient, rendered as an open-ended list of subjective and objective findings, been adequately described? Is a candidate clinical syndrome (e.g., "amnesic dysnomic aphasia," line 4), with its own embedded uncertainties about what "usually" happens, a useful and reliable description? Is the relative location of structures in The Brain a trustworthy guide for locating difficulties in a particular (and inaccessible) brain? Uncertainty about descriptions of particular situations in relation to generalizations is endemic in clinical medicine, as in most other areas of technical or scientific practice (Engeström, Engeström, & Karkkainen, 1995; C. Goodwin, 1994; Hall, 1998; Hall & Stevens, 1996; Lynch, 1990, 1995).

In this wayfinding episode, the flip chart is a central resource for overcoming uncertainty, particularly as it sits between the activities of students and their faculty coach. By analyzing their activity closely (see the Pursuing the Hippocampus Across Representational Media subsection), we can follow how this technical object is brought into coordination with talk and action to help locate the cause of trouble in a particular patient's brain. This part of the analysis moves forward in time, showing how agreed-on "representational states" (Hutchins, 1995a, p. 49) are assembled. However, what happens if we try to move in the other direction? What if we take the flip chart showing sectional views of an idealized brain and follow its developmental trajectory into the past (i.e., we de-[in]scribe the work of constructing this object)?

Fortunately, Star (1985, 1989) has already done this, studying 19th-century clinical researchers and how they managed uncertainty while trying to construct generalized brain maps very similar to the flip chart used in this PBL session. Given widely varying instances of brain trauma, nonstandard clinical methods, and the spotty data that typically resulted, how could these researchers develop a general theory that maps observable psychological functions (and their disruption) onto brain structure? Based on an analysis of historical records, Star showed they did this (in part) by simplifying or deleting variations encountered among individual brains as they constructed graphical maps (or flip charts) that rendered The Brain (again, my term) from a localizationist perspective. Particularly relevant to Betty's theorizing, Star (1989) reports 19th-century strategies for filtering cases that are "classic" or "perfect" for teaching purposes (pp. 72–73).

A more general treatment of the construction of "boundary objects" appears in Star and Griesemer (1989), who argued that these objects are "both plastic enough to adapt to local needs and the constraints of the several parties employing them, yet robust enough to maintain a common identity across sites" (p. 393). As an ideal type, the flip chart reflects past-time activities of selection, deletion, and simplification in clinical research; in prospective use, this chart (and The Brain it represents) must be actively mapped back onto particular brains. The work of managing uncertainty does not disappear, it simply reverses direction as a matter of making versus using the abstraction.

Whether we run the analysis forward or backward in time, we find that the work of having a theory is a distributed achievement. Star (1989) described the context of developing a localizationist theory (that Betty and her colleagues presume):

At no one point in time or space can a piece of scientific evidence, or even the work or beliefs of one scientist, be said to represent a theory in its entirety. Instead, theories are actions distributed over multiple sites and long periods of time. No central authority evolves, adjudicates, or disseminates theories. (p. 62)

For example, while finishing this article, I found the following front-page story in *The San Francisco Chronicle*, "Brain Lesions Can Spark Cravings for Fine Food: Disorder Called 'Gourmand Syndrome'" (May 20, 1997). Corroborating Star's account, the work of having a theory about localization continues.

In summary, Betty's theories would be very difficult to mount without the prior, historical development of localizationist theory for brain structure and function. Star's (1989) analysis helps us to see the missing masses brought together in medical texts and the flip chart used by Betty and her colleagues; this nicely complements our efforts to follow their work in using this abstraction during the PBL session.

Representing Jake's Brain in Relation to The Brain

The result of this wayfinding episode is a shared assembly representing the relative location of structures in a three-dimensional, generic brain. In the course of having a theory, Betty and her colleagues assemble a representational state that supports judgments about plausible vascular causes in a particular brain. They construct this state in response to an instructional request (i.e., the Coach asks, "Where is the hippocampus," line 16), and their difficulties indicate there is confusion across students about the location of generic brain structures (e.g., Norman's selection of the temporal lobe, Jenny's loss of memory, and Lill's nonspecific identification of "white matter" in a frontal section). My interpretation of the episode is that assembling this representational state (i.e., the relative location of brain structures in three-dimensional space) is necessary for achieving a shared understanding of Betty's first theory.

State in hand, Betty then turns to "My other theory" (line 69) and uses this jointly assembled representation (i.e., "right there in the area we were pointing to," lines 71–73) to propose a space-occupying lesion. Meeting resistance from Maria, Norman, and the coach, she again starts navigating in assembled three-dimensional space (e.g., the "posterior part of the posterior li:mb," lines 87–88). I do not follow this in my analysis, but it is important to note that (a) these complex assemblies recur in the work of having a theory, (b) they are open to analysis as important phenomena for research in distributed cognition, and (c) these analyses can follow learning and teaching as a matter of ongoing relevance in multiparty talk.

COMPARING CASES OF THEORY BUILDING

Question 2: What can comparative analysis tell us about the development of discipline-specific representational practices across settings in which people are said to be having a theory?

I next want to compare activity across settings and raise questions about the development of practices for having a theory. The setting for comparison is the presumably "everyday" character of dinnertime conversations among people who are described as "English-speaking, Caucasian-American families" (Ochs et al., 1992, p. 37). Ochs et al. provided a wonderfully provocative analysis of "storytelling as a theory-building activity" (p. 37), conducted over a corpus of recordings that target 5-year-old children interacting with older siblings and parents while they eat dinner. As Ochs et al. pointed out, telling stories is a common type of narrative activity across a wide range of settings (e.g., M. H. Goodwin, 1990; Linde, 1993; Orr, 1996).

Storytelling as a Theory-Building Activity

People make different kinds of contributions when they conarrate a story, and in Ochs et al.'s (1992) analysis these include: Abstracts, Settings, Initiating Events (IE), Internal Responses to IE, Attempts to deal with IE, Consequences, and Reactions. When the story centers on a problem and its actual or possible solution (i.e., an IE that provokes Internal Responses and Attempts), then conarrators work to frame events as an "explanatory sequence" (p. 45). In these sequences, a problematic event leads to further, complicating actions, resulting events (Consequences), and protagonists' Reactions to those events.

Labov's (1972) earlier description of narrative syntax and how it can be used to transform personal experience strongly complements some of Ochs et al.'s (1992) claims. In particular, Labov argued that narrative syntax (or form) can be used to "intensify" selected events as relevant, to "compare" actual events with others that might have occurred, to "correlate" or superimpose events onto one another (i.e., to articulate relative conditions for action), and to "explicate" the point or conclusion of a story (p. 392). Also relevant to Ochs et al.'s analysis of theory building among young children, Labov compared narratives across age levels and suggested that complex forms of evaluation (e.g., comparators) develop late:

> The skilled adult complicates his representation of experience, moving back and forth from real to imaginary events. Children complain, question, deny, and worry, but adults are more aware of the significance of this activity and more likely to talk about it. (p. 396)

As Ochs et al. pointed out, more complex contributions to storytelling may be handled (or scaffolded) by older members of the family.

Ochs et al. (1992) argued that stories become a theory-building activity when conarrators challenge and revise the facts (IEs and Consequences), methods (Attempts), or ideology (Responses and Reactions) that make up an explanatory sequence. Ochs et al. borrowed this description of challenges from Laudan's (1984) account of scientific discourse. Latour (1987) made a similar argument, relating the stability of scientific or technical claims to the cost of opposing them (i.e., how a dissenter could mobilize a challenge to facts, methods, or ideology). Under a successful challenge, the structure of an explanatory sequence can change, and conarrators can take up new perspectives on the events under discussion.

Most important for development, children who participate as conarrators in these narrative activities experience an "opportunity space" in which they can learn "skills critical to engagement in the world of theory" (Ochs et al., 1992, p. 38). These skills include (a) perspective taking, (b) understanding stories as "versions" or "theories" that can be revised (Ochs et al. called this "metacognition"), (c) using analytic thinking to evaluate different perspectives, and (d) reworking or reframing the perspectives of protagonists or conarrators in (or of) the story (Ochs et al. called this "theory-reconstruction"). In the corpus of dinnertime stories that Ochs et al. analyzed, relatively simple theory-building exchanges were typical: Explanations involved a single past-time event, challenges were to third-party protagonists' methods (i.e., conarrators produced present-time Reactions to past-time Attempts), and revisions contributed future-time alternatives (Attempts) for dealing with problematic events.

Theory Building in the "Chili Peppers Story"

This is a rich framework for thinking about the interactional work of having a theory, whether at family dinner tables or in medical schools. I briefly present an example of a "story as theory" from Ochs et al.'s (1992) article, then use this as a comparative basis for picking similar phenomena out of Betty's opening presentation.

The "Chili Peppers Story" (see Ochs et al., 1992, pp. 43–44) is initiated by an older sibling (Oren, a boy, age 7) and conarrated by his mother. The father and "target child" (Jodie, a girl, age 5) are also present, and the story appears to be produced at least in part for the benefit of the younger child. In my excerpts from the "Chili Peppers Story" and in my comparative analysis of Betty's presentation, I list Ochs et al.'s categories for contributions in bold italics just before the utterance they describe. In each case, I make inferences that go beyond Ochs et al.'s original report, but I have tried to use these categories in ways that are consistent with that report. I have also preserved the orthography of Ochs et al.'s transcription conventions as much as possible.

Oren starts the story when he hears that the guacamole they are eating contains chili peppers. After pretending to die in his chair, Oren frames the narrative events as "funny" (Reaction), but his mother disagrees, challenging this account and providing another ideological frame ("no that wasn't funny"). Oren then turns to his younger sister (the target child) and says:

Setting and Initiating Event

Oren: yeah I was two:? - and then you know what happened? - ((*to Jodie*))
        I ate that chili pepper? .h ((*imitating action of eating it*)) and Mom
        thought it was a bean? - and I ate it?
        Consequence₁
        and I burned to death ((*turns to Mom*)) - what hap?pened. -what=
        Consequence₂

Mother: =You burnt your mouth
        (1.2) ((*Oren and Mom looking at each other*))

Apparently, the ideological challenge is still underway because Oren's mother reframes "burned to death" as "burnt your mouth" (i.e., Consequence₁ vs. Consequence₂). Oren then asks if he had to go to the hospital (i.e., an Attempt to deal with this IE, not shown here) and again elicits a less extreme alternative event from his conarrator:

Attempt₂

Mother: We gave you ice
Oren: where
Mother: in your mouth
        Reaction
Oren: oh: my god - How long did I - keep it in
Mother: (a few minutes)

After asking about his Response to the burning and ice (he asks "Did I love it?" and Mom tells him he cried), Oren loudly exclaims "YOUR FAULT" and reaches over to touch his mother's cheek. As we reach the end of the "Chili Peppers Story" (or Ochs et al.'s, 1992, report of it), Mom's redrafting of the events as being serious ("that wasn't funny") appears to have been successful. Following this new ideological frame, Oren begins to retaliate (a present-time Reaction) as his sister looks on and laughs:

Jodie: hhh ((*soft laugh—at Oren's moves toward Mom?*))
        Reaction
Mother: I thought it was ((*Oren now pinching both of Mom's cheeks*)) a um
        -green pep?per -.HHHHH - ((*pulling Oren's hands away*)) OW that
        really hurts honey?
Oren: your fault - (I get to do whatever I want to do once)

In Ochs et al.'s (1992) analysis, the "Chili Peppers Story" is an example of theory building in at least three senses. First, Oren and his mother conarrate an explanatory sequence in which a pepper is mistaken for a bean, resulting problems are encountered (i.e., Oren burned his mouth, was hurting, and cried), and a solution is found (i.e., ice in Oren's mouth). Although Ochs et al. do not mention it, this resolution may be important for the present-time situation in that Jodie, a similarly inexperienced and potential future-time protagonist, is eating guacamole that contains peppers. Second, Mom challenges Oren's initial framing of the story as "funny," redrafting the ideological status of these events within the family. Mom also challenges Oren's dramatic descriptions of Consequences (e.g., burning to death vs. burning his mouth) and Attempts (e.g., going to the hospital vs. putting ice in his mouth). Therefore, her challenges reorganize the explanatory sequence of the "Chili Peppers Story" in a way that balances Oren's competing interpretations (i.e., both funny and drastic). Third, these conarrated redraftings turn a funny situation into one in which a child is allowed (or believes himself to be allowed) to retaliate against a parent for a past-time mistake.

If Oren and his mother have constructed a theory, what is the theory about, in the sense that 19th-century localizationists had a theory about brain function or that Betty has a theory about the cause of slurred speech in an elderly male patient (i.e., a vascular lesion)? Ochs et al. (1992) do not pose this question, but I will list several alternatives before revisiting Betty's theories in Ochs et al.'s terms. If we ask where the conarrators in the "Chili Peppers Story" make or use claims for generality or necessity, several different theories appear plausible:

1. Mom redrafts Oren's contributions into a theory about *how to handle spicy food with young children*. Mistakes happen, children burn their mouths and get upset, but these problems can be solved with ice and comforting. These events are not funny, but they are also not life threatening.

2. With help from his mom, Oren assembles a theory of *dealing with spicy food* for his younger sister, Jodie. Parents sometimes feed you things that will burn your mouth, so you need to be careful what you eat. Things that look like green beans merit special attention. If you do burn your mouth, your parents can help and you will get better.

3. Oren takes Mom's redrafting as an opportunity to construct (or strengthen) a theory about *family discipline*. You can retaliate against someone when you suffer from a mistake that is their fault. This is true regardless of whether they are a child or a parent, and you "get to do whatever [you] want to do once."

Betty's Theory as a Storytelling Activity

If Ochs et al.'s (1992) analysis and broader developmental claims about theory-building skills are correct, then we should be able to identify the same types of conarrated contributions in the narrative organization of Betty's theory. With some open-ended interpretive allowances, I think it is possible to describe Betty's theories in similar terms. To make this mapping visible, I re-present the extended turn comprising Betty's first theory (lines 1–14, including others' utterances) using Ochs et al.'s descriptive categories, again listed in bold italics before the utterance they describe.

> ***Abstract/Setting***
>
> Betty/Text: See, what it said in here n-<u>my</u> theory
>
>   ⌜ about this
>
> | ***Reaction***
>
>   ⌞ <u>khu</u>-(.hhhh)
>
> Betty/Text: amnesic (.) dysnomic aphasia? (0.6) um it
>
> ***Initiating Event₁***
>
> Betty/Text/Maria: says the cause of lesion is usually deep
>
>   in temporal lobe just like Maria was
>
>   saying

The Abstract/Setting is given by a hybrid Initial Teller (Betty/Text). By calling Betty/Text a *hybrid*, I mean to describe the way in which speakers selectively assemble resources like medical texts, flip charts, and prior talk to make a contribution during conversation. This sense of hybridization follows what Callon and Law (1995, p. 494) called a "material gradient" between person and text (i.e., representational form). Along this gradient, forms offer structure but do not determine human action (i.e., hybrids create a "discretionary space" for action). Hybrid agency, as actually achieved in conversation, is strongly similar to various accounts of the dialogic character of discourse (Bakhtin, 1981; Hanks, 1996, pp. 201–225; Palincsar, 1999/this issue; Wertsch, 1991).

Before Betty's contribution can even be completed, however, a male speaker (I hear Norman) begins the work of conarration with what may be a challenge (i.e., his explosive breath or laughter, coincident with Betty/Text's use of "theory"; see Glenn et al., 1999/this issue). I have also categorized this as a reaction, placing his utterance within the set of contributions that build Betty/Text's story. In the wake of the male speaker's negative assessment (C. Goodwin & Goodwin, 1992), the Initial Teller expands to include more voices (Betty/Text/Maria) and contributes the first Initiating Event₁ (IE₁): the "cause of lesion" is located "deep" in the temporal lobe in amnesic dysnomic aphasia.

> ***Consequence***
>
> Betty/Text: presu<u>m</u>ably interrupting
>
>   connections of <u>sensory</u> speech areas with
>
>   the <u>hippocampal</u> and <u>para</u>hippocampal
>
>   regions. (1.0)

Reaction
Betty: and I think the hippocampus
         is like a lot more medial
Consequence
Betty: so if it was affecting that area
Initiating Event₂

Betty: it might be the
         ┌ anterior cerebral circulation.
         │ *Reaction*
Norman: └ Anterior.

Betty/Text's next contribution is the functional Consequence of IE₁ within the brain (i.e., an interruption of sensory speech areas). After a pause, this is followed by Betty's own comparative Reaction, in which she challenges the Text by arguing that the hippocampus is deeper in the brain (i.e., "I think the hippocampus is like a lot more medial"). Betty challenges the location of a lesion (IE₁) causing the disruption, not the proposal that there is a disruption (Consequence). Restating this Consequence as a conditional given (i.e., "if it was *affecting* [italics added] that area"), she proposes an alternative Initiating Event₂ (i.e., vascular trouble in the "anterior cerebral circulation"). Latching onto the culminating contribution of Betty's first theory, Norman gives a more positive Reaction, this time expressed as a cocompletion of Betty's utterance (i.e., "Anterior").

In closing this account of Betty's theory as a storytelling activity, it is important to note that talk about problems in her hybridized narrative has shifted from Jake's complaints to a structural disruption in the functional organization of a generic brain. That is, the hybrid I call Betty/Text/Maria is narrating a general-purpose story about what happens in The Brain, and it appears that recipients of this theory will accept a general description of a disease process (i.e., a vascular lesion affecting the hippocampus) in place of and as an explanation for the difficulties reported by a particular patient. It is in this sense that Betty's theory rests on and extends the line of work that Star (1989) described among 19th-century localizationists.

THE DEVELOPMENT OF DISCURSIVE
PRACTICES FOR HAVING A THEORY

This brief analysis of Betty's first theory about a vascular lesion could be extended to her "other theory" of a space-occupying lesion (lines 69–120), in which her peers and the coach successfully challenge matters of fact (e.g., line 79) and methods of diagnostic inference (e.g., line 104). Pursuing this analysis would be productive, but my point is only to show that problem-based medical instruction and dinnertime conversations can both be described as theory-building activities.

Following Schegloff's (1992) principle of procedural consequentiality, I have not used taken-for-granted differences between a children–parents group and a medical students–faculty group to claim that they possess different kinds of logic or different powers of observation. Extending this principle to include aspects of developmental consequentiality, I have shown that, in both settings, more experienced participants (i.e., the coach and Oren's mom) work to reorganize the accounts given by less experienced participants (i.e., medical students and Oren). In doing this analysis, I avoided using settings called "family dinners" and "medical school" as sociological givens that explain away potentially relevant similarities and differences. The result is a form of comparative analysis that opens up new possibilities for studying development by not disqualifying children and their parents from the work of having a theory. Ochs et al. (1992) made a similar argument:

> To **elevate** the cognitive processes that posit and evaluate scholarly theories and **dismiss** those that posit and evaluate everyday theories would be a disservice to both, mystifying the realm of scholardom and underappreciating how family and other everyday discourse practices socialize metacognitive, metalinguistic processes as instincts that scientists and other scholars depend on. The two realms are not so far apart. (pp. 66–67)

If we refuse to let given aspects of people or settings prefigure the analysis and instead follow the details of discursive practice, what develops? One possibility is that we face the apparent paradox of producing (in the analysis) interchangeable social actors. That is, as we theorize the work of having a theory in terms of procedural consequentiality, do we make Oren and his mom interchangeable with Betty and her coach? This is the paradox that I mentioned in the beginning of this article (see the Following Developmental Trajectories for Having a Theory section), and we now have some comparative material for considering whether this is (a) a crisis for close studies of talk in interaction or (b) a promising start towards rebalancing studies of the organization and development of technoscientific competence. To consider these alternatives, we need to look carefully at the relevant similarities and differences between these two cases of having a theory.

How Are Dinnertime and Medical School Conversations Alike?

How is Betty's first theory, given with help from the Text, Maria, and Norman in the context of explaining findings for a particular patient, similar to the "Chili Pepper Story" by Oren and his mother, given in the context of explaining how ingredients in guacamole can cause trouble? The list of what I take to be important similarities includes the following.

1. Both cases involve *multiparty contributions to stories about problems,* offered in small groups by participants who are familiar with each other.

Oren, Mom, and Jodie (as a relatively passive recipient) talk about eating hot food. Betty, textbooks, other students, the coach, and The Brain are all involved in talk about brain lesions and associated symptoms.

2. Both problem-solving narratives include *explanatory sequences.*

Oren and his mother talk about the effects of mistaking chilies for green beans (e.g., "I burned to death") and different treatments for this condition (i.e., hospitalization vs. sucking on ice). Betty and her colleagues talk about lesions in particular areas of the brain (e.g., "anterior cerebral circulation," line 14) as the cause of specific behavioral symptoms.

3. In both conversations, people *challenge matters of fact, method, or ideology.*

Mom challenges Oren's account of the facts (e.g., was the mistaken object a pickle or a bean?), the methods used (e.g., did Oren go to the hospital or get ice?), and his ideological perspective on these (e.g., was this funny or not?). Despite all this, Oren manages to challenge his mother's methods for feeding her children. Betty challenges the Text's factual account of where a lesion might be located (i.e., "deep in temporal lobe," lines 5–6, vs. "a lot more medial," line 12). Later, Maria and the coach challenge Norman's initial attempt to locate the hippocampus in the flip chart. Challenges to facts and methods are even more dense in the context of Betty's second theory (e.g., Maria's question about the extent of leg involvement at lines 79, 82, and 85).

4. Both narratives also show evidence for *redrafting causal accounts.*

Oren takes up his mother's ideological reframing (i.e., "no that wasn't funny") to carry off an attempt at retaliation (i.e., pinching her cheek and announcing, "I get to do whatever I want to do once"). Norman abandons his initial location for the hippocampus during the wayfinding episode, and Betty's second theory is abandoned after challenges from Maria, the coach, and Norman.

5. Participants also conarrate *aspects of generality* in both cases.

Oren narrates the past-time "Chili Pepper Story" in the context of present-time trouble with eating guacamole. By juxtaposing these events, he proposes a comparison that could be consequential for Julie (i.e., she may avoid guacamole or sift through it carefully). In addition, after appropriating various contributions by his mother, Oren arrives at (or reproduces) a general statement about family relations (e.g., the conditions under which retaliation is allowed). Betty and her colleagues use the generic location of structures and their functional correlates in The Brain to identify the source of trouble in an elderly patient's particular brain.

6. Both narratives involve *asymmetric participation structures* in which more knowledgeable members scaffold contributions by less knowledgeable members.

Oren starts his story for the apparent benefit of his younger sister, then his mother challenges and redrafts his contributions to create an account of eating hot food that is both more serious and less drastic than Oren's initial telling. Betty proposes two theories, and she is treated by her peers and the coach as the author of these theories. However, the coach also appropriates her contributions and challenges by her peers to initiate and structure teaching and learning events (i.e., the wayfinding episode, as an anatomical lesson about The Brain and its representation in technical language and orthographic projection).

Comparative Analysis and the Crisis of Interchangeability

This is a healthy dose of similarity, and it lends support to Ochs et al.'s (1992, p. 67) claim that family and academic discourse are "not so far apart." However, these similarities also lead to an apparent paradox. When we compare the specific practices through which talk, action, and inscription are coordinated to do things like theory building, how do we avoid describing people and settings in language that makes them (at least in theory) interchangeable? In the comparative analysis undertaken in this article, there is evidence to support Ochs et al.'s argument that Oren's conversation with his mother might develop into an activity that resembles Betty's presentation of theories. In what principled way, however, are these activities different? If we stop the comparative analysis of having a theory at this point, what is to keep us from sending Betty's patient (Jake Elwood and his complaints) to Oren's house for a diagnostic consultation while sending Oren (or Julie) to be raised by medical students and their faculty coaches?

I call this a *crisis of interchangeability*, because, in trying to make inferences about what is common across these fragments of conversation (i.e., analytic generalizations for describing what develops), my analysis actively suspends taken-for-granted differences between the activities of ordinary people and technoscientists. This is precisely what Schegloff's (1992) principle of procedural consequentiality encourages us to do because relying on extrinsic characterizations of types of people or contexts risks reproducing existing cultural beliefs about cognition, activity, and society.

For a similar analytic strategy in a comparative study that suspends and then restores differences between grade school children and civil engineers, see Hall and Stevens (1995). This approach treats the "infinite regress" of potentially relevant contexts (Cicourel, 1992, p. 309) as an analytical tool, selectively restoring broader layers of context (e.g., extending time and place) in an attempt to question or disrupt asymmetric allegations of competence or incompetence. Latour (1987, chap. 5), following Bloor (1976), makes a similar recommendation for symmetry when studying how scientists' knowledge claims become true or false. Sociologists of science beg questions about knowledge production when they asymmetrically assign responsibility for "true" theories to nature and "false" theories to faulty thinking or social bias. The parallel with Schegloff (1992) is that developmental studies of talk in interaction should not explain competence or expertise (e.g., in technoscientific practice) on the basis of who people "are" (e.g., a child vs. a medical student) or where they "sit" (e.g., at a dinner table or in a classroom).

Thus far, the comparative analysis in this article focuses on categories that are demonstrably relevant to the conduct of activity. These include (a) assembling representational states, (b) present- and past-time resources for managing uncertainty, (c) mapping specific cases onto generic idealizations, (d) conarrating explanatory sequences, (e) challenging accounts (i.e., of facts, methods, or ideologies), and (f) redrafting explanations. However, if dinnertime stories and medical school theorizing are strongly similar across these categories, what is left to develop? There must also be differences if something is to develop, and these will show up as absences when one activity system is compared with another (e.g., absent materials, types of activity, or types of organization).

We can escape the crisis of interchangeability only by restoring what is absent or different across these cases of having a theory. Studying the absence of something, however, places considerable strain on the principle of demonstrating procedural consequentiality. That is, how can we study development without taking a perspective on competence that lies outside the conduct of activity thought to produce that development (i.e., describing relevant similarities and differences across settings for activity)? This is a difficult, metatheoretical problem, and I think it accounts for why so few close studies of talk in interaction ask comparative questions about learning or development. Although a growing collection of studies focus on how talk in interaction supports learning within specific settings (C. Goodwin, 1993a; Hutchins, 1995a; Jacoby & Gonzales, 1991; Ochs et al., 1994), relatively few studies compare learning or development across different work settings (C. Goodwin, 1994; Hall & Stevens, 1996; Lave & Wenger, 1991) or across school and work settings (Hall & Stevens, 1995; Stevens & Hall, 1998).

Because this kind of comparison is the purpose of this article, I turn now to a description of differences between the work of having a theory in dinnertime and medical school conversations.

How Are Dinnertime and Medical School Conversations Different?

What are the relevant differences between these two cases of having a theory, and how would they keep us from sending elderly patients out to family dinners or children to medical school? Drawing on the comparative analysis presented earlier, I describe two differences that seem particularly important for the development of discursive practice.

1. *Technologies used to represent phenomena* under discussion are very different across these cases.

Oren and his mother discuss the problems associated with eating hot food, but there is no Text on chili peppers and what happens when you eat them, no flip chart showing the structural organization of "The Guacamole" or "The Mouth," and no specialized but broadly conventional technical language for finding one's way around food or the process of eating it. From what Ochs et al. (1992) reported (and in my own experience), none of these materials are necessary for having a theory in dinnertime conversation. In considering what needs to develop to enable theory building of the sort that Betty is doing, this is a striking absence.

These representational technologies are all present for Betty and her colleagues, although they by no means use them fluently. As I argued earlier (see the Coordinating Talk and Action With Inscription subsection), assembling a representational state that will support having a theory about brain lesions requires bringing these technologies into coordination. Some of the resources for doing this in medical school are also available to Oren and his mother (e.g., narrative, gesture, and gaze), but the technical "massification" of theorizing in medical school is substantially more complicated. For example, what would happen if Betty and her colleagues lost access to the Text, the flip chart, or the medical history of Jake Elwood? At least for the purposes of problem-based teaching and learning, I suspect they would find it very difficult to assemble and use idealized versions of The Brain to do clinical decision making. Latour (1996b; see also Engeström, 1996; Lynch, 1996) made a similar argument about how technologies frame human interaction and enable increasingly "complicated" forms of collective activity. The work done by Betty and her colleagues to map Jake's brain onto The Brain is an excellent illustration of Latour's point.

2. The *scope and generality of claims* made in each case are also very different.

Both fragments of conversation involve aspects of generality in the sense that conarrators compare events and shift their accounts of these events (or their significance) in time (past, present, future), place (there, here, anywhere), and agency (exclusive self, inclusive speaker or recipient, anyone). For example, while pinching his mother's cheeks at the end of the "Chili Peppers Story," Oren counters her protest by shifting into future time and describing a general rule ("I get to do whatever I want to do once"). Although these narrative resources are common to both conversations, they are used to do very different things.

There is no sense in which Oren's or his mother's claims about managing spicy food or family relations are as broad ranging as corresponding claims about structure and function in The Brain. For participants in this PBL fragment, a specific instance (Jake Elwood) can be understood by mapping it onto a collection of technical materials (i.e., texts and the flip chart) that they treat as an idealized, trans-situational generalization. This approach to explanation is enabled by what I earlier called the massification of medical practice with technical forms of representation that bring many instances of a "syndrome" to bear on explaining some particular instance.

I use *generalization* because Betty and her colleagues treat the location of generic brain structures (e.g., the hippocampus), the circulatory system that supplies these structures, and the behavioral functions governed by these structures as an adequate account of difficulty in some particular brain. As such, The Brain that they interactively assemble is taken to cover all possible brains (i.e., it is trans-situational). Particular representations such as the flip chart also work as abstractions in the sense that they selectively delete material that designers judge to be irrelevant or counterproductive for their use (e.g., the skull, neck vertebrae, and surrounding soft tissues have all been stripped away). When Betty joins forces with the Text to propose "amnesic dysnomic aphasia" (line 4), she contributes a crowd of particular cases, smoothed and combined into a syndrome through processes of selection and deletion (Star, 1989) to start the work of having a theory.

In this sense, the scope of Betty's claim is enormous, simultaneously ranging over (a) all these other cases of this syndrome contributed in the past-time work of clinical researchers and (b) the community of medical practitioners that would treat the Text (i.e., Harrison's text on pathology) and the flip chart as authoritative generalizations. In contrast, when Oren joins forces with his mother to tell a story about eating a chili pepper, mobilization and the scope of claims have a much smaller range.[3] These are, perhaps, obvious differences between dinnertime conversation and medical consultations, but they are, in many respects, what the discursive practices of technoscience are about.

There are other contrasts to consider (e.g., the extent to which these conversations are organized as teaching events), but the relative levels of massification

---

[3]Two reviewers of this article pointed out that cultural practices surrounding hot or spicy food may rival or even exceed the technical massification and scope or generality of Western medicine. This would be interesting to pursue, but I will leave the high-end salsa market and Scoville pepper ratings to others for now. One of these reviewers also suggested that Oren might be developing into a parent rather than (or as well as) into a technoscientist.

and generality in these cases provide ample reason for keeping Jake Elwood and Oren in their respective positions. In my view, these differences are critical to understanding how explanation, challenge, and generality are conducted when learners begin to participate in technical and scientific practices. Dinnertime storytelling provides early opportunities for learning to give accounts of life experiences, but there is ample room for further development along these lines.

CONCLUSIONS

This article explores the organization and development of discursive practices for having a theory, starting with a fragment of PBL instruction (the shared record for this special issue) then turning to a comparison with Ochs et al.'s (1992) analysis of theory building in dinnertime conversations.

A close analysis of the PBL fragment shows that having a theory requires deliberate (and often collective) effort by people, both in the present-time conduct of activity (e.g., in conversations) and in the past-time work of others who have created enduring, technical objects. Betty, her peers, and their coach need to coordinate talk, embodied action, and a variety of inscribed representations to do the work of having a theory. The analysis moves forward in time to follow how people bring these different resources into coordination to assemble shared representational states (see the Having a Theory About a Vascular Lesion and Pursuing the Hippocampus Across Representational Media subsections). Directing the analysis backward in time (see the Present- and Past-Time Resources for Managing Uncertainty subsection), I briefly follow the historical development of conventional representational forms (e.g., maps or charts of The Brain) and again find people working to assemble representational states and to manage uncertainty. Combining both lines of analysis (i.e., inscription in present time and de-[in]scription in past time), we can begin to account for the layered character of making and using representations in technoscientific practice (C. Goodwin, 1995; Hall & Stevens, 1995, 1996; Hutchins, 1995b; Ochs et al., 1994). This kind of analysis is revealing when, within these representational practices, we find evidence for how generality, necessity, and authority are actually achieved. Although I have not pursued these phenomena very deeply in this article, I hope to have demonstrated that it is feasible to undertake this kind of analysis and that we can learn a great deal by doing so.

Comparing the work of having a theory across medical school and dinnertime conversations (see the Comparing Cases of Theory Building section) yields an impressive collection of similarities. These include (a) assembling representational states, (b) collaborating with others to manage uncertainty, (c) mapping specific events onto general accounts of how things work, (d) conarrating explanatory sequences, (e) challenging the accounts of narrative protagonists and other speakers, and (f) revising one's own account in response to the perspectives and challenges of others. In these descriptive terms (see the How Are Dinnertime and Medical School Conversations Alike? subsection), people in both fragments of conversation (i.e., the medical students–faculty coach group and the children–parents group) appear to be building theories of events that interest them.

Without paying close attention to differences between these fragments, it is difficult to decide what might develop in the narrative activities of theory building. I describe this as a crisis of interchangeability (see the Comparative Analysis and the Crisis of Interchangeability subsection) for developmental research that is conducted on the basis of a close analysis of talk in interaction. Attempting to demonstrate that analytic categories (e.g., the similarities listed earlier) are procedurally consequential for the conduct of the conversations being compared, it is possible to overlook differences that are important for development. Particularly in comparative research, finding developmentally relevant differences may require analytic perspectives that extend beyond the mutually accountable methods used by participants in specific situations.

Comparing medical school and dinnertime conversations also reveals important differences (see the How Are Dinnertime and Medical School Conversations Different? subsection). The availability and use of conventional technologies for representing events is one of these, and the relative absence of this in dinnertime conversations shows one line of development. There are also important differences in the scope and generality of accounts produced in these two fragments of conversation to the extent that clinical decision making (i.e., the context for Betty's theories) can be described as a problem of mapping particular instances onto heavily instrumented generalizations. These two differences, alone, effectively dissolve any apparent crisis of interchangeability.

Finally, the kind of comparative research outlined in this article is increasingly appealing for several reasons. First, this research moves outside of classrooms or laboratories as privileged (or dominant) sites for doing, learning, and teaching the practices of technical or scientific work. I am not arguing that we should abandon these settings as places in which people learn, only that we should be willing to consider a wider range of settings when studying the development of discursive practices like having a theory. Second, and from a design-oriented perspective on educational research, it is very encouraging to find technical or scientific features in the activities of ordinary people while at the same time discovering the organization of ordinary, embodied work in the activities of technoscientists. Identifying points of contact between everyday and scientific understanding opens up new possibilities for teaching and learning. For example, comparative findings from this kind of research (both similarities and differences) might encourage closer attention to the material infrastructure of settings (and their histories) as central resources for competence. An analysis of how these distributed forms of competence are organized and how they develop will require careful attention to how people and things act collectively.

ACKNOWLEDGMENTS

This article was undertaken with support of a National Academy of Education/Spencer Foundation postdoctoral fellowship to study changing representational practices in mathematics across instructional settings. The link to clinical medicine is remote and much facilitated by Tim Koschmann. The ideas in this article reflect ongoing conversations with Jim Greeno, Susan John, Susan Newman, Leigh Star, Reed Stevens, Tony Torralba, and Karen Wieckert. I am also indebted to helpful critical comments on the manuscript by Aaron Cicourel, Phil Glenn, Jay Lemke, and Ricardo Nemirovsky. None of these people should be held responsible for what I say here.

REFERENCES

Akrich, M. (1992). The de-scription of technical objects. In W. Bijker & J. Law (Eds.), *Shaping technology/building society: Studies in sociological change* (pp. 205–224). Cambridge, MA: MIT Press.

Atkinson, P., & Delamont, S. (1977). Mock-ups and cock-ups: The stage-management of guided discovery instruction. In P. Woods & M. Hammersley (Eds.), *School experience: Explorations in the sociology of education* (pp. 87–108). New York: St. Martin's Press.

Bakhtin, M. M. (1981). *The dialogic imagination: Four essays* (M. Holquist, Ed., and M. Holquist & C. Emerson, Trans.). Austin: University of Texas Press.

Barrows, H. S. (1994). *Practice-based learning: Problem-based learning applied to medical education.* Springfield: Southern Illinois University School of Medicine.

Berg, M. (1997). Of forms, containers, and the electronic medical record: Some tools for a sociology of the formal. *Science, Technology, & Human Values, 22,* 403–433.

Bloor, D. (1976). *Knowledge and social imagery.* London: Routledge & Kegan Paul.

Brain lesions can spark cravings for fine food: Disorder called "gourmand syndrome." (1997, May 20). *San Francisco Chronicle,* p. A1.

Callanan, M., Shrager, J., & Moore, J. L. (1995). Parent–child collaborative explanations: Methods of identification and analysis. *The Journal of the Learning Sciences, 4,* 105–129.

Callon, M., & Law, J. (1995). Agency and the hybrid collectif. *The South Atlantic Quarterly, 94,* 481–508.

Cicourel, A. V. (1992). The interpenetration of communicative contexts: Examples from medical encounters. In A. Duranti & C. Goodwin (Eds.), *Rethinking context: Language as an interactive phenomenon* (pp. 291–310). Cambridge, England: Cambridge University Press.

Cronon, W. (1992, March). A place for stories: Nature, history, and narrative. *The Journal of American History,* pp. 1347–1376.

diSessa, A. A., Hammer, D., Sherin, B., & Kolpakowski, T. (1991). Inventing graphing: Metarepresentational expertise in children. *Journal of Mathematical Behavior, 10,* 117–160.

Engeström, Y. (1996). Interobjectivity, ideality, and dialectics. *Mind, Culture, and Activity, 3,* 259–265.

Engeström, Y., Engeström, R., & Karkkainen, M. (1995). Polycontextuality and boundary crossing in expert cognition: Learning and problem solving in complex work activities. *Learning and Instruction, 5,* 319–336.

Glenn, P. J., Koschmann, T., & Conlee, M. (1995). Theory sequences in a problem-based learning group: A case study. In J. L. Schnase & E. L. Cunnius (Eds.), *Proceedings of CSCL '95: The first international conference on computer support for collaborative learning* (pp. 139–142). Mahwah, NJ: Lawrence Erlbaum Associates, Inc.

Glenn, P. J., Koschmann, T., & Conlee, M. (1999/this issue). Theory presentation and assessment in a problem-based learning group. *Discourse Processes, 27,* 119–133.

Goodwin, C. (1981). *Conversational organization: Interaction between speakers and hearers.* New York: Academic.

Goodwin, C. (1993a, November). *The blackness of black: Color categories as situated practice.* Paper presented at a conference on Discourse, Tools and Reasoning: Situated Cognition and Technologically Supported Environments, Lucca, Italy.

Goodwin, C. (1993b). Recording human interaction in natural settings. *Pragmatics, 3,* 181–209.

Goodwin, C. (1994). Professional vision. *American Anthropologist, 96,* 606–633.

Goodwin, C. (1995). Seeing in depth. *Social Studies of Science, 25,* 237–274.

Goodwin, C., & Goodwin, M. H. (1992). Assessments and the construction of context. In A. Duranti & C. Goodwin (Eds.), *Rethinking context: Language as an interactive phenomenon* (pp. 147–189). Cambridge, England: Cambridge University Press.

Goodwin, M. H. (1990). *He-said-she-said: Talk as social organization among black children.* Bloomington: Indiana University Press.

Hall, R. (1998). Following mathematical practices in design-oriented work. In C. Hoyles, C. Morgan, & G. Woodhouse (Eds.), *Studies in mathematics education series: Vol. 10. Rethinking the mathematics curriculum* (pp. 29–47). London: Falmer.

Hall, R. (in press-a). *Making mathematics on paper: Toward an ecological theory of quantitative inference.* Mahwah, NJ: Lawrence Erlbaum Associates, Inc.

Hall, R. (in press-b). Video recording as theory. In A. Kelly & D. Lesh (Eds.), *Handbook of research design in mathematics and science education.* Mahwah, NJ: Lawrence Erlbaum Associates, Inc.

Hall, R., & Stevens, R. (1995). Making space: A comparison of mathematical work in school and professional design practices. In S. L. Star (Ed.), *The cultures of computing* (pp. 118–145). London: Basil Blackwell.

Hall, R., & Stevens, R. (1996). Teaching/learning events in the workplace: A comparative analysis of their organizational and interactional structure. In G. Cottrell (Ed.), *Proceedings of the 18th Annual Conference of the Cognitive Science Society* (pp. 160–165). Mahwah, NJ: Lawrence Erlbaum Associates, Inc.

Hanks, W. F. (1996). *Language and communicative practices.* Boulder, CO: Westview.

Heath, S. B. (1991). "It's about winning!" The language of knowledge in baseball. In L. Resnick, J. Levine, & S. Teasley (Eds.), *Perspectives on socially shared cognition* (pp. 101–124). Washington, DC: American Psychological Association.

Hutchins, E. (1995a). *Cognition in the wild.* Cambridge, MA: MIT Press.

Hutchins, E. (1995b). How a cockpit remembers its speeds. *Cognitive Science, 19,* 265–288.

Jacoby, S., & Gonzales, P. (1991). The constitution of expert–novice in scientific discourse. *Issues in Applied Linguistics, 2,* 149–181.

Jordan, B., & Henderson, A. (1995). Interaction analysis: Foundations and practice. *The Journal of the Learning Sciences, 4,* 39–103.

Labov, W. (1972). The transformation of experience in narrative syntax. In W. Labov (Ed.), *Language in the inner city* (pp. 354–396). Philadelphia: University of Pennsylvania Press.

Latour, B. (1987). *Science in action: How to follow scientists and engineers through society.* Cambridge, MA: Harvard University Press.

Latour, B. (1992). Where are the missing masses? The sociology of a few mundane artifacts. In W. Bijker & J. Law (Eds.), *Shaping technology/building society: Studies in sociological change* (pp. 225–258). Cambridge, MA: MIT Press.

Latour, B. (1996a). *Aramis or the love of technology.* Cambridge, MA: Harvard University Press.

Latour, B. (1996b). On interobjectivity. *Mind, Culture, and Activity, 3,* 228–245.

Latour, B., & Woolgar, S. (1979). *Laboratory life: The construction of scientific facts.* Princeton, NJ: Princeton University Press.

Laudan, L. (1984). *Science and values.* Berkeley: University of California Press.

Lave, J., & Wenger, E. (1991). *Situated learning: Legitimate peripheral participation.* New York: Cambridge University Press.

Lemke, J. L. (1999/this issue). Typological and topological meaning in diagnostic discourse. *Discourse Processes, 27,* 173–185.

Levinson, S. C. (1992). Activity types and language. In P. Drew & J. Heritage (Eds.), *Talk at work* (pp. 66–100). Cambridge, England: Cambridge University Press.

Linde, C. (1993). *Life stories: The creation of coherence.* New York: Oxford University Press.

Lynch, M. (1990). The externalized retina: Selection and mathematization in the visual documentation of objects in the life sciences. In M. Lynch & S. Woolgar (Eds.), *Representation in scientific practice* (pp. 153–186). Cambridge, MA: MIT Press.

Lynch, M. (1991). Method: Measurement—Ordinary and scientific measurement as ethnomethodological phenomena. In G. Button (Ed.), *Ethnomethodology and the human sciences* (pp. 77–108). Cambridge, England: Cambridge University Press.

Lynch, M. (1995). Laboratory space and the technological complex: An investigation of topical contextures. In S. L. Star (Ed.), *Ecologies of knowledge: Work and politics in science and technology* (pp. 226–256). Albany: State University of New York Press.

Lynch, M. (1996). DeKanting Agency: Comments on Bruno Latour's "On interobjectivity." *Mind, Culture, and Activity, 3,* 247–251.

McNeill, D. (1992). *Hand and mind: What gestures reveal about thought.* Chicago: University of Chicago Press.

Musen, M. A., Wieckert, K. E., Miller, E. T., Campbell, K. E., & Fagan, L. M. (1995). Development of a controlled medical terminology: Knowledge acquisition and knowledge representation. *Methods of Information in Medicine, 34,* 85–95.

Ochs, E., Jacoby, S., & Gonzales, P. (1994). Interpretive journeys: How physicists talk and travel through graphic space. *Configurations, 1,* 151–171.

Ochs, E., Taylor, C., Rudolph, D., & Smith, R. (1992). Storytelling as a theory-building activity. *Discourse Processes, 15,* 37–72.

Orr, J. (1996). *Talking about machines: An ethnography of a modern job.* New York: ILR Press.

Palincsar, A. S. (1999/this issue). Applying a sociocultural lens to the work of a transition community. *Discourse Processes, 27,* 161–171.

Schegloff, E. A. (1992). On talk and its institutional occasions. In P. Drew & J. Heritage (Eds.), *Talk at work* (pp. 101–134). Cambridge, England: Cambridge University Press.

Star, S. L. (1985). Scientific work and uncertainty. *Social Studies of Science, 15,* 391–427.

Star, S. L. (1989). *Regions of the mind: Brain research and the quest for scientific certainty.* Stanford, CA: Stanford University Press.

Star, S. L. (1995). The politics of formal representations: Wizards, gurus, and organizational complexity. In S. L. Star (Ed.), *Ecologies of knowledge: Work and politics in science and technology* (pp. 88–118). Albany: State University of New York Press.

Star, S. L., & Griesemer, J. R. (1989). Institutional ecology, "translations" and boundary objects: Amateurs and professionals in Berkeley's museum of vertebrate zoology, 1907–39. *Social Studies of Science, 19,* 387–420.

Stevens, R., & Hall, R. (1998). Disciplined perception: Learning to see in technoscience. In M. Lampert & M. Blunk (Eds.), *Talking mathematics in school: Studies of teaching and learning* (pp. 107–149). Cambridge, England: Cambridge University Press.

Wertsch, J. (1991). *Voices of the mind: A sociocultural approach to mediated action.* Cambridge, MA: Harvard University Press.

Williams, S. M. (1992). Putting case-based instruction into context: Examples from legal and medical education. *The Journal of the Learning Sciences, 2,* 367–427.

DISCOURSE PROCESSES, 27(2), 219–230

COMMENTARIES

What Difference Does the Difference Make? Understanding Difference Across Perspectives

Judith L. Green
Graduate School of Education
University of California, Santa Barbara

Marleen McClelland
Department of Physical Education
Youngstown State University

In this discussion, we examine how theory–method relations shape what could, and could not, be known about problem-based learning (PBL) through the different approaches to discourse analysis used. We show how, by reading and analyzing the articles as a collective body of work rather than as individual articles, we created a telling case, one that makes previously obscure theoretical relations between theory and method suddenly apparent (Mitchell, 1984, p. 239). Using an ethnographic perspective, we make visible what these articles individually and collectively contribute to our understanding of discourse analysis and to the study of the processes of knowledge construction in PBL contexts. We also describe factors contributing to the challenge we found in reading and understanding these different analyses and how these factors led us to question how our own interests, theoretical background, and preference for a particular research approach influenced our interpretations.

In this discussion, we present a cross-case approach to the analysis of the articles in this special issue that makes visible how theory–method relations shape what

---

Correspondence and requests for reprints should be sent to Judith L. Green, Graduate School of Education, University of California, Santa Barbara, CA 93106. E-mail: green@education.ucsb.edu

could, and could not, be known about problem-based learning (PBL). We show how, by reading and analyzing the articles in this special issue as a collective body of work rather than as individual articles, we created a telling case, one that makes previously obscure theoretical relations suddenly apparent (Mitchell, 1984, p. 239). Specifically, we discuss issues of theory–method relations raised across the articles to make visible what difference the differences in discourse analysis approach make to those of us interested in the study of learning in problem-based contexts.

TOWARD A FRAMEWORK
FOR EXPLORING COMMONALITIES
AND DIFFERENCES ACROSS ARTICLES

To frame how we see the issue as a telling case and what we see as "telling" about these articles, we draw on recent arguments in anthropology, educational ethnography, and philosophy of science. Specifically, we draw on conceptual arguments about ethnographically based case studies in cultural anthropology (Ellen, 1984; Mitchell, 1984), the study of the history of scientific knowledge within the sciences (Toulmin, 1972), and philosophic arguments about the ex-pressive potential of a research language (Strike, 1974). Furthermore, we describe how an ethnographic perspective (Green & Bloome, 1997) provided the basis for exploring the theories guiding each study as well as how the authors' purpose for each analysis shaped method, findings, and knowledge claims.

ADOPTING AN ETHNOGRAPHIC PERSPECTIVE:
ON WAYS OF READING THE ARTICLES
AS CULTURAL ARTIFACTS

To make visible what these articles contribute to our understanding of discourse analysis and to the study of the processes of knowledge construction in PBL contexts, we approached each guided by an ethnographic perspective. Green and Bloome (1997) argued that, by adopting an ethnographic perspective, it is possible to explore the cultural knowledge that members of a group need to know, un-derstand, produce, and predict to participate in the "bit" of life recorded on a video record or in a graphic or written text (see also Gee & Green, 1998). Building on this argument, we began our analysis by asking ethnographic questions drawn from cultural anthropology: Who can say or do what, to and with whom, when, where, under what conditions, in relation to what artifacts, for what purposes, in what ways, with what outcomes? By asking this context-sensitive question, or linked chain of questions, we were able to situate our analysis in the author(s)' arguments and actions; that is, to construct an emic perspective on theory–method relations as represented in each article. Through this analysis, we were able to construct an understanding of how the author(s)' theoretical framework(s) led to the selection of particular angles of vision on the social world recorded on the 6-min video segment; particular relationships among actors in the problem-based setting; and particular processes, practices, and outcomes. By examining the logic of inquiry used by each researcher (or team of researchers), we were able to identify to varying degrees the theoretical assumptions and principles of research guiding their work. This knowledge of theory–method relations is needed to identify the knowledge required to use each approach (Birdwhistell, 1977; Gee & Green, 1998).

Although we view the entire set of articles as an important collection with both variety of perspectives and theoretical explication, we were not able to access all articles equally. Two factors contributed to the problems of access. These will be addressed before we discuss how the collection as a whole informs the study of PBL. First, and possibly most obvious to readers, the author(s) provided varying degrees of information and definition. Some assumed more shared knowledge about the theoretical underpinnings of their work than others, placing a greater burden on us as readers than we expected. The challenge we found in reading and understanding these different analyses led us to question how much of the tension we felt as readers was due to the author(s)' lack of articulation and how much was due to our own interests, theoretical background, and preference for a particular research approach.

The answer to this question came when we considered the conditions under which these articles were written and how those conditions influenced what could be presented. The authors all engaged in a common task—analyzing the same 6-min segment of video from a PBL project. By holding the data set constant and providing differing analyses on that data, the authors laid a foundation for a comparative analysis that made visible the potential of each approach for analyzing PBL events. However, we found that the comparative analysis did not lead us to select one perspective over another. Rather, at times the comparisons made visible what particular authors meant and how the question asked shaped data selected and analysis undertaken. The comparison also made visible fine-grained similarities and differences among perspectives, differences that shaped what we could know, understand, and produce. We also found our knowledge of theory–method relations was enhanced as we moved across articles, reflected back on each, and considered what questions could be asked.

The common task, however, also proved to be a limitation because the author(s) did not select these data from their own bodies of research, set their own questions for this research, or have an opportunity to request further information or collect further data. Although all authors focused on the data made available and presented illustrative findings, several also pointed to the need for additional data (e.g., over-time data, historical data, and interview data, among others). This information about missing data or other analyses that were needed was important to gaining a fuller understanding of the potential of each approach. Having pointed this out, we would like to add one caveat. Given the task provided and the limits of space, the omission of information on additional data valued does not mean that such information was not valued by those who did not explicitly include a discussion of the need for such data.

The acknowledgment of missing data does not diminish what can be seen through these analyses. Each article is an illustrative case (Ellen, 1984) of the potential for the approach, not an all-inclusive one. From this perspective, the collective set, when read comparatively in light of the conditions under which the articles were generated, constitutes a telling case (cf. Mitchell, 1984) in that it makes visible previously obscured information, information not available within a single article or perspective. Having arrived at this understanding, we decided on a strategy of raising general issues rather than restating the arguments of individual authors or pointing to issues not addressed within individual studies.

The second difference that influenced the sense that we made of the individual and collective articles came from the differences in interpretation and reading that each of us had of particular articles or content dimensions of articles. Although we share a common theoretical and methodological orientation grounded in ethnography and interactional sociolinguistics, we engage in research using this framework in different professional settings and have different areas of interest that influence what and how we read and interpret particular perspectives and articles. Marleen McClelland is a faculty member in physical therapy in a College of Health and Human Services at Youngstown State University, whose research focuses on discourse of interprofessional teams in medical settings (McClelland & Sands, 1993; Sands & McClelland, 1994). Judith Green is a faculty member in teaching and learning in The Graduate School of Education at the University of California, Santa Barbara, whose research focuses on issues of equity of access and the social construction of knowledge in classroom settings with linguistically diverse students (e.g., Green & Bloome, 1997; Santa Barbara Classroom Discourse Group, 1992; Tuyay, Floriani, Yeager, Dixon, & Green, 1995). Our common theoretical framework provided a way of exploring the articles in a systematic manner; the differences in professional interest and background knowledge became resources for examining the substantive content and theoretical perspectives across the different analyses.

The differences in background knowledge, experience, and interest allowed us to make certain issues visible that the other did not see. For example, Marleen was sensitive to how the different authors identified, took up, and interpreted medically specific language; how they engaged in medically oriented reasoning practices; and how they interpreted the medical students' knowledge about the case provided. The transcription of a medical term in two ways, *corticospinal* and *cortical spinal,* in the version of the manuscripts we reviewed, was meaningful to Marleen. The use of *corticospinal* as a single word suggested to her that the author was familiar with medical terminology in ways that the use of two words would not have signaled. From her experience within health sciences and medical settings, she saw the single term as a representative of the "technical language" of the medical community. Judith did not share Marleen's expertise and background knowledge and had no way of assessing which of these inter- pretations was more or less appropriate for medical students seeking to be taken as professionals, not merely as students. In other words, Marleen had insider knowledge of medicine that served as a resource for her as she read, interpreted, and assessed the different approaches, findings, and claims. Thus, this small difference was "telling" to her but not to Judith.

This small difference raised questions about how the naming of a term marks the researcher as knowledgeable to those in particular communities of practice (e.g., medicine). However, in discussing this issue, we identified a second caveat. It was not possible to determine whether the researchers had heard the term differently, and we could not determine whether they had been given a transcript with the term written one way and then had changed it based on their hearing of the interaction. Given the lack of information provided on transcribing, we were unable to assess whether the interpretation of one researcher being "more knowledgeable about medical terms" was accurate. What is important to note is not whether one was more accurate but rather the issue that the contrast raises— small differences in the transcripts provided these scholars made a difference in interpretation and made one appear knowledgeable to particular communities and less knowledgeable to others (see Green, Franquíz, & Dixon, 1997).

Another telling example of how difference in background knowledge of the researcher influences what can be seen, interpreted, and made visible occurred when we examined the different theoretical frameworks represented in these articles. Authors across the articles referred to concepts introduced or perspectives taken from particular fields of study or disciplinary bases (e.g., conversation analysis [CA], applied linguistics, semiotics, sociocultural psychology, and seman- tic analysis, among others). For example, differences in the ways in which CA was taken up and used by two different sets of authors (Glenn et al.; Hall) became telling for Judith. As one who teaches courses on qualitative research methods, she has been "listening in" on an ongoing argument on an Internet discussion group (a list-serve) for those interested in CA. The argument in this community centers around what counts as CA, and whether using CA for other purposes is the same as doing CA. The difference in this discussion centers on whether an analysis contributes to the field of CA. Those concerned with this aspect of the argument see CA not as mere method but as a field of study (cf. Atkinson & Heritage, 1984). Others seek to use the insights gained from this field and the methods developed to explore questions beyond those of interest to conversation analysts. The articles in this issue are examples of the latter approach.

To understand why this issue is important and how it is a telling case raised by these articles, recent work on the history of scientific knowledge by Toulmin (1972) needs to be considered. Toulmin set out to explain the stability and change in the growth of scientific knowledge. He viewed science as a dynamic process in which theories, presuppositions, and representational devices (models, diagrams, etc.) evolve over time. He argued that disciplinary knowledge shows continuity and coherence in the short term and that an extended period of time is needed to see radical changes in concepts. Analysis of Toulmin also shows that his view of conceptual change is based on a theory of rationality of science in which science is viewed, not as a universal set of inference rules or commitments to central theories but as a collective set of commonly held concepts, practices, and actions of members of a group called "scientists." Thus, for those who see themselves as conversation analysts, the issue is not one of method separate from purpose, tenets of evidence, and agreed-on practices.

From this perspective, those seeking to apply CA do not have the same goals or tenets of evidence or the same commitment to the development of CA as a field. Thus, they break the norms that members of the CA community adhere to and ask questions of little interest to that community. Although some may view this as an issue of ownership, Toulmin's (1972) argument allows us to see that it is more than that. While application may be valuable, as both the articles in this issue show (Glenn et al.; Hall), the researchers applying these perspectives, methods, and approaches do not share the questions that are of interest to those within CA. The tension of what counts within a discipline is not the same as the issue of value of the perspective to other disciplines or research communities for their questions. However, we raise this tension to make visible issues of criticism that may be leveled as we take up the traditions of others and seek to use them for our own questions (for a parallel set of concerns, see Heath, 1982; Rist, 1980).

ON THE EXPRESSIVE POTENTIAL
OF A RESEARCH LANGUAGE: TOWARD
A PRODUCTIVE APPROACH TO A CRITICAL DIALOGUE

In the previous section, we raised cautions, tensions, and issues that became visible as we sought ways of examining the contributions of each article and argued for viewing the collection as a whole as the telling case (for a similar argument across perspectives on classroom research, see Green et al., 1996). In this section, we suggest the power of the multiple lenses represented in the collective articles and construct an argument about the expressive potential created by bringing together a set of complementary perspectives—perspectives that share a common conceptual orientation (i.e., the social construction of knowledge; cf. Green & Harker, 1988). To construct this argument, we introduce one final concept, the notion of the expressive potential of a research language (Strike, 1974), and then use it to point to similarities and differences across perspectives represented in the articles. Our goal is to show how understanding the expressive potential of the different traditions represented by these articles leads to the potential for developing an interdisciplinary approach with a conceptually coherent, enhanced expressive potential as well as to an understanding of what information is lost when particular perspectives are not considered.

To illustrate how the language or discourse of a discipline or research perspective shapes what members count as meaningful research questions, goals, hypotheses, and educational phenomena, Strike (1974) analyzed behaviorist theory and practices. Strike argued that the particular vocabulary of behaviorism was overly restrictive in that "there are meaningful and possibly true assertions about educational goals and methods which cannot be asserted in its vocabulary" (p. 104).

Strike's (1974) argument suggests that the choice of language by members of a particular tradition places limits on what can be discussed and what aspects can be described in and through that research language. His argument also suggests that the choice of language, with all its related conventions for use, inscribes a particular view and set of understandings about the phenomena under study and entails particular ways of engaging in research. From this perspective, it is necessary to view each research tradition as constituting and being constituted by a theoretical language with a set of related practices. In other words, we can speak of the discourse of behaviorists, of other schools of research, and of traditions within education, as well as the discourse of science or of medicine (for an analysis of the discourse of medicine, see Mishler, 1984). Viewed in this way, there is no single discourse of medicine or, in this instance, PBL. There are only discourses of medicine or of PBL used by different groups for particular purposes. One of those discourses is the discourse of our research tradition. In proposing the concept of expressive potential, Strike provided a conceptual approach to exploring the potential of any given discourse in relation to particular issues of concern to researchers, educators, and policymakers (for a related discussion on the relation between conceptual perspectives and language use, see Bazerman, 1987; Lakoff & Johnson, 1980).

The authors of the articles in this issue make visible the relation between their theories and their research; and, in so doing, provide insights into their expressive potential. However, when we juxtaposed the different perspectives, by asking the ethnographic questions presented in the earlier section of this discussion, we found subtle as well as explicit distinctions that were not visible in the individual articles. To identify potential areas in which different perspectives can be productively brought together and to make visible the limits of different perspectives, we present two types of comparative information. In the first part of this discussion, we show commonality of themes and directions across sets of the articles. This analysis makes visible how different analytic perspectives provide both common and unique information. Following that, we reverse the process and explore what would be lost if a particular perspective were not considered. Both discussions are illustrative, not comprehensive, and we apologize in advance for the reduction of the complex arguments found in each article.

One theme identified across the articles is the notion that PBL events, processes, and practices are both similar to and different from "ordinary" situations involving problems. One way of seeing the similarities and differences, of seeing how the ordinary becomes extraordinary in a PBL context, is in the work of Hall. Hall explicitly contrasts how having a theory is constructed in two contrasting situations: a dinner table conversation and the PBL segment on the 6-min videotape. Through this contrast, he makes visible how purpose, roles and relationships, and context of situation shape how a theory is constructed, what is available to be taken up or constructed as theory, and how having a theory is socially constructed. He also shows how members of a conversation negotiate what counts as "having a theory."

Using the processes, practices, and foci we identified in the Hall article, we examined whether others talked about similar phenomena and, if so, how they did this, what types of questions they asked, and what could be known. We found that each of the authors use contrast as a key to understanding the phenomena of interest; yet, what was contrasted and what served as the focus of the analysis varied. For example, most of the authors contrast the student role with the coach's (or, in Hall's case, the mother's) role. Across the articles, we gained insights into different dimensions of the coach's role, including (a) making certain that particular people did not dominate (Glenn et al.), (b) keeping the macrostructure going while making visible the knowledge needed to participate (Frederiksen), (c) seeding the conversation at important points to support students in trying on and learning medical discourse (Palincsar), (d) balancing the theory proposed by the child/student (Hall), (e) and shaping or privileging particular forms of language—that is, typological (Lemke). Although these do not exhaust the range of contrasts, they do illustrate how each perspective frames a particular phenomenon, views roles and relationships among actors in particular ways, and points to particular actions as valued.

Across these articles, authors, through such contrasts, point to and make visible the existence of dual agendas in a conversation (e.g., parent–child, teacher–student, student–student). Authors also identified multiple demands facing participants (e.g., personal, interpersonal, and collective/community), factors contributing to the complexity of task (e.g., participating in a local event while simultaneously using the event to learn how to be a member of a larger community of practice), and the need of participants to process simultaneously different semiotic systems (e.g., visual semiotic cues and verbal semiotic cues).

As Lemke points out, these agendas and processes are simultaneous; yet, for analytic purposes, they need to be separated. The analytic separation of phenomena and the need to reintegrate them is also addressed by the authors. Through multiple approaches to phenomena, through the use of different levels of analysis, and through the juxtaposition of different actors' points of view, the authors identify ways that analytic integration and separation can be addressed. Although the approaches were often similar in that they were complex and did not rely on single measures or instruments, what was explored differed across studies. For example, Glenn et al. provide insights into the sequential nature of theory construction. Their analysis shows how members constructed a situated view of what counted as having a theory by making visible the sequential actions of members, by exploring which actions were taken up and worked with, and by exploring which failed to be taken up and acknowledged. Similarly, Hall presents evidence of how members constructed situated views of what counts as having a theory.

Although these two sets of authors (Glenn et al.; Hall) focus on a common process, and even select common transcript segments to analyze, they do so using different languages, which, at times, overlap and at other times, diverged. When we contrasted the different languages used, we found that Glenn et al. focus primarily on applying a CA approach and language, whereas Hall draws on constructs from this perspective and combines them with other perspectives (e.g., applied linguistics). This difference was not merely one of discourse; it also led to differences in method, units of observation, and analytic processes. Each of these articles, then, provides particular information and insight into the process involved in having a theory. Glenn et al. provide insights into the iterative process of practice and to the notion of distributed cognition. Hall provides a language to talk about and insights into the relations among time, setting, and materials. He also raises issues about the "missing masses"—that is, how technoscience practices focus on analytic generalizations (e.g., the brain) rather than localized views (Thomas's brain) with all its complexity and variation. He also raises questions about the role of cultural artifacts in the conversation (e.g., flip charts) and how they inscribe particular abstract views of phenomena.

The issue of the charts and relationships among members was also of interest to others in this collection. Both Frederiksen and Palincsar, drawing on different theoretical perspectives on cognition and development, also show how knowledge is interpersonally constructed, leading to specific ways of acting, thinking, and being (e.g., to what Frederiksen called collaborative reasoning, in contrast to personal reasoning). Both authors raise questions about how students learn the reasoning, language, and practices of the more experienced professionals or community. These questions lead them to different levels or types of analyses, ones that move between the collective and the individual to examine what was available to be taken up as well as what counted as knowing, doing, and being a member. In this way, they enhance our understanding of what counts as knowledge within particular communities and how such knowledge is constructed through the interactions and actions among members.

The richness of these individual illustrative cases and the languages they provide cannot be explicated fully in a brief discussion. The examples presented do not provide a full understanding of the expressive potential of any one of these articles. Space does not permit careful or detailed explication of the value of each. Therefore, to illustrate the value of these articles, we have elected to end this discussion by briefly describing what could not be seen, asked, or understood should a particular perspective be taken away or omitted. To frame the argument, we begin with a common assumption across all articles—that knowledge is socially constructed within a particular context, by a particular group, engaging in particular activity for particular purposes, with particular outcomes for the group as well as for individual members. What we subtract is not all that a perspective or article provides but rather a key element, process, or phenomena.

For example, Palincsar introduces the notion of a language of communities. Her analysis allows us to see different types of communities and to conceptualize the task of medical students as one of learning the language, processes, and practices of a community. In doing this, she provides a language about community and communities that offer a way of viewing the progression of medical students as one of moving from being members of a transitional community to being members of a particular community of practice. If we remove her theoretical language, we lose the ability to discuss issues of boundaries between communities, identity as constructed within a particular community, and other issues involved in becoming a member of particular communities. If we remove Glenn et al. and Hall, we weaken our ability to show how particular practices of a group are constructed through sequential activity. If we subtract Frederiksen's perspective, we lose ways of following and representing the chain(s) of reasoning being developed, the relations between collective and individual reasoning, and the propositional content made available through collective interactions and textual artifacts. If we then take away Lemke's language on semiotic systems, we lose ways of talking about the multiple semiotic systems that members draw on and use to make sense at particular times in developing activities. By not considering the types of semiotic systems that are drawn on or privileged (or both), we run the risk of privileging verbal interactions while simultaneously ignoring other cue and semiotic systems that members use.

With each language we subtract, we also lose the methodological approaches, the ability to ask and explore particular questions, and the levels of analysis that add texture, point of view, angle of vision, and explanatory power. In other words, we lose the expressive potential of each research language. However, if we can find ways to engage in multidisciplinary approaches or to create more complex research approaches, then we can enhance the expressive potential of our work. As the articles in this special issue show, this will be a complex task in and of itself, for no one group of researchers can use all perspectives simultaneously and all are not appropriate to answer all questions. There is a need for particular perspectives to examine specific domains or to explore particular phenomena and questions.

For those of us seeking to tie research and practice together so that research can inform practice and practice can inform theory development, these articles show us that we can no longer claim that one perspective holds the key. Rather, what the articles show is that we need to build a conceptually coherent approach to enhancing the expressive potential of our research programs. Finally, this collection shows the value of comparative work using common data to make visible the expressive potential of different theoretical positions. Such work will provide the basis for the critical discourse being called for by philosophers of science, for as Longino (1990) argued:

> Scientific knowledge . . . is an outcome of the critical dialogue in which individuals and groups holding different points of view engage with each other. It is constructed not by individuals but by an interactive dialogic community. A community's practice of inquiry is productive of knowledge to the extent that it facilitates transformative criticism. (p. 112)

By viewing the articles as a collective, and by considering what each contributes and what would be lost if the perspective were not considered, we illustrated one way that a positive, transformative, and generative critical dialogue can be undertaken. From this perspective, one way to view the power of these articles and the work of the authors in exploring a common data segment is to see them as providing a model for how future critical dialogues can be undertaken.

ACKNOWLEDGMENTS

We thank Ginger Weade, of Ohio University, and Carol Dixon, of the University of California, Santa Barbara, for their editorial comments.

REFERENCES

Bazerman, C. (1987). Codifying the social scientific style: The APA publication manual as a behaviorist rhetoric. In J. S. Nelson, A. Megill, & D. N. McClosky (Eds.), *The rhetoric of the human sciences* (pp. 125–144). Madison: University of Wisconsin Press.

Birdwhistell, R. (1977). Some discussion of ethnography, theory, and method. In J. Brockman (Ed.), *About Bateson: Essays on Gregory Bateson* (pp. 103–144). New York: Dutton.

Ellen, R. F. (Ed.). (1984). *Ethnographic research: A guide to general conduct.* San Diego: Academic.

Gee, J., & Green, J. L. (1998). Discourse, literacy and social practice. In P. D. Pearson (Ed.), *Review of research in education* (Vol. 23, pp. 119–169). Washington, DC: American Educational Research Association.

Green, J. L., & Bloome, D. (1997). Ethnography and ethnographers. In S. B. Heath, J. Flood, & D. Lapp (Eds.), *Handbook for research in the visual and communicative arts* (pp. 181–202). New York: Macmillan.

Green, J. L., Franquíz, M., & Dixon, C. (1997). The myth of the objective transcript. *TESOL Quarterly, 31,* 172–176.

Green, J. L., & Harker, J. (1988). *Multiple perspective analyses of classroom discourse.* Norwood, NJ: Ablex.

Green, J. L., Kelly, G. J., Castanheira, M. L., Esch, J., Frank, C., Hodel, M., Putney, L., & Rodarte, M. (1996). Conceptualizing a basis for understanding: What differences do differences make? *Educational Psychologist, 31*, 227–234.

Heath, S. B. (1982). Ethnography in education: Defining the essentials. In P. Gillmore & A. A. Glatthorn (Eds.), *Children in and out of school: Ethnography and education* (pp. 33–55). Washington, DC: Center for Applied Linguistics.

Lakoff, G., & Johnson, M. (1980). *Metaphors we live by.* Chicago: University of Chicago Press.

Longino, H. E. (1990). *Science as social knowledge: Values and objectivity in science inquiry.* Princeton, NJ: Princeton University Press.

McClelland, M., & Sands, R. G. (1993). The missing voice in interdisciplinary communication. *Qualitative Health Research, 3*, 74–90.

Mishler, E. (1984). *The discourse of medicine.* Norwood, NJ: Ablex.

Mitchell, J. C. (1984). Case studies. In R. F. Ellen (Ed.), *Ethnographic research: A guide to general conduct* (pp. 237–241). San Diego: Academic.

Rist, R. C. (1980). Blitzkrieg ethnography: On the transformation of method into a movement. *Educational Researcher, 9*(2), 8–10.

Sands, R. G., & McClelland, M. (1994). Emic and etic perspectives in ethnographic research on interdisciplinary teams. In E. Sherman & W. J. Reid (Eds.), *Qualitative research in social work* (pp. 32–41). New York: Columbia University Press.

Santa Barbara Classroom Discourse Group. (1992). Constructing literacy in the classroom: Literate action as social accomplishment. In H. Marshall (Ed.), *Redefining learning: Roots of educational change* (pp. 119–151). Norwood, NJ: Ablex.

Strike, K. A. (1974). On the expressive potential of behaviorist language. *American Educational Research Journal, 11*, 103–120.

Toulmin, S. (1972). *Human understanding: The collective use and evolution of concepts.* Princeton, NJ: Princeton University Press.

Tuyay, S., Floriani, A., Yeager, B., Dixon, C., & Green, J. (1995). Constructing an integrated, inquiry-oriented approach in classrooms: A cross case analysis of social, literate and academic practices. *Journal of Classroom Interactions, 30*(4), 1–15.

DISCOURSE PROCESSES, 27(2), 231–240

Transitioning to Professional Practice: A Deweyan View of Five Analyses of Problem-Based Learning

Jeremy Roschelle
SRI International
Menlo Park, California

The collection of five articles analyzing an episode of problem-based learning (PBL) in a medical school is rich with conversation, mediating objects, and layered intentions of the participants. Video proves itself to be a medium that can provide common ground to a thoroughly encompassing set of perspectives in discourse analysis, ranging from Vygotskian to cognitive theories, linguistic to sociotechnical orientations, and concerns both local to PBL and fundamental to the social sciences. Beyond merely exploring methodological possibilities, the five articles can be seen to take an important first step toward resolving a critical issue of learning theory, which was first articulated by John Dewey: How do we understand the boundary between commonsense and technical forms of reasoning, action, and discourse? By what means do students grow from everyday to specialized forms of practices? This collection suggests a possible resolution to this issue through multidisciplinary, layered, and nuanced discourse analysis.

This special issue presents a conversation of a rare form: Several experts have joined forces to analyze a single strand of human activity from diverse perspectives. The strand of activity, an episode of problem-based learning (PBL) in a medical school, is rich with conversation, mediating objects, and layered intentions of the participants. Although each of the experts engages in discourse analysis, their perspectives range widely from Vygotskian to cognitive theories, linguistic to sociotechnical orientations, and concerns both local to PBL and fundamental to the social sciences.

In seeking to read these five articles as a coherent conversation, one might look for a coherent issue each author is addressing, a resolution under debate, or a possible synthesis arising from the dialectic. The articles, however, quite

---

Correspondence and requests for reprints should be sent to Jeremy Roschelle, SRI International, 333 Ravenswood Avenue, Menlo Park, CA 94025. E-mail: roschelle@acm.org

thoroughly foil an impulse toward seeking consensus on any particular issue in the science of discourse or the study of PBL. Each author has picked a different issue or problem to address with these data. Glenn, Koschmann, and Conlee, for example, choose to focus on showing that the participants orient themselves to this episode as being about theories. Frederiksen is working toward "a generalizable cognitive theory of PBL" (p. 139). For Lemke, the medium is the message; he draws out the analytic problems and opportunities that arise from choosing video as the data medium. Palincsar focuses on identifying the kind of community these participants constitute. Finally, Hall uses these data and others to draw out a paradox with potentially ruinous consequences for the theory of discourse.

The authors share the conventions of discourse analysis but appear to occupy their theoretical (or some might say, ideological) space alone. Frederiksen, for example, is solitary in his quest for an encompassing cognitive theory. Hall is equally alone in his framework of comparative development. Lemke seems oriented to linguistics proper, whereas Palincsar suggests a Vygotskian frame. Of these, only Frederiksen seems to expect that the ultimate result of these conversations might be a grand theory. In fact, for apparent lack of a common problem to resolve, one might take the absurdist position that the emperor has only clothes—each analyst is dressing up this video excerpt with his or her favorite style of garment, and through their mastery of tailoring arguments, hiding the fact that the data means nothing.

Contrary to the absurdist view, each analyst has brought a long-standing theme of their own research program to bear on quite unfamiliar data. (In fact, the data was likely collected without a prior intention to offer it to this collection of analysts.) Consider for a moment how amazing this is: In most preceding forms of recording, data points were already reduced to meet the needs of a particular analytic perspective by the time they hit the recording medium; after the fact, the only comparative analyses possible were those that accept the same presumptions about the form of encoding. This almost always narrowed the set of possible interpretations. For example, in this set of articles, conventional encoding of the data as a transcript would have denied Lemke and Hall access to the participants' use of gestures and material objects. Likewise, a conventional transcript might have removed some of the subtleties of more articulate or more concealed fluency that enabled Palincsar to see this group as a transitional community.

Moreover, it is remarkable just how deeply the perspectives of each researcher connect with this data. Each researcher takes up the challenge of "procedural consequentiality" (Schegloff, 1992), as discussed in Hall's article. That is, each analyst endeavors to show how the concepts they use are also concepts that the participants attended to. These analyses do not apply merely because this is a PBL session, or in a medical school, or around a table. Indeed, there is quite compelling evidence that the participants themselves find the analytic concepts essential in their enactment of the PBL discourse. For example, Palincsar finds markers of a transitional community in the way the female participants in each setting modulate their articulateness. Quite clearly, Palincsar is not the only one who sees this; the participants themselves attend to changes in articulateness and its resulting impression on the speaker's authority or belonging. Similarly, Lemke's typology–topology tension seems fairly instrumental in the progress of the group: Norman attends to power of topology in deliberately moving from his seat to a position in front of the chart, and the coach seems equally purposeful in directing students toward categorical reasoning. Frederiksen introduces the concept of discourse macrostructure, and the diagnostic procedure frame in particular, and shows that the coach orchestrates discourse to fit this frame.

Thus, these articles move to bring diverse theoretical ideas into mutual engagement. Although the move is but a first foray, success can be claimed on at least one dimension: Video proves itself to be a medium that can provide common ground to a throughly encompassing set of perspectives. The triumph of the video medium here is that each author has managed to bring a substantial body of prior research into contact with an unfamiliar data excerpt in ways that are substantive and enlightening. In this collection of articles, we see video enable the transfer of theory to new contexts without the usual investment in adapting data collection techniques.

At the very least, reading different analyses of the same data reveal more clearly the differences among the approaches. For example, the sequential, local character of Glenn et al.'s conversation analysis stands out against the hierarchical propositional analysis that Frederiksen's cognitive orientation encourages. Both their articles are similar, however, in attempting a more comprehensive treatment of the data, whereas Hall, Lemke, and Palincsar each take a more thematic and selective approach. Although the identification of similarities and differences could continue on for pages, more interesting issues lurk beneath the surface. Indeed, although the authors do not seem to engage in a common theoretical sphere or to have agreed in advance to seek convergent outcomes, they do find similar issues emergent in the data. The differential emphasis of their perspectives, although not directly competing to give an account of the data, do illuminate these shared concerns.

In what follows, I seek to bring one set of emergent issues to light by imposing a point of view on the conversation. That is, rather than directly contrast the analysts to each other—a task that is nearly impossible given their widely varying orientations—I attempt to portray the analyses against a fixed point of reference, John Dewey's philosophy.

CONNECTIONS TO DEWEY

Dewey (1916) comes to mind first for his educational philosophy. PBL is surely an intellectual descendant of the project-based pedagogy Dewey advocated. The role of the coach, as facilitator and guide, and the immersion in a simulation of professional activity mirror the kind of progressive reforms for which Dewey is best remembered. In addition, Dewey comes to mind as the first philosopher to take communities of practice as a unit of analysis and to focus on practical deliberations that result in judgments of what to do next. Indeed, like many of the analysts here, *practice* is Dewey's (1938) primary unit of analysis of technoscientific activity: "The conduct of scientific inquiry, whether physical or mathematical, is a mode of practice; the working scientist is a practitioner above all else" (p. 161). Medicine, of all professions, probably best exemplifies the interplay of disciplined reasoning and timely decision making that Dewey sought to extend to all human pursuits.

Dewey (1938) connected to this episode at a deeper level as well, for "having a theory" also evokes his central philosophical concept: the pattern of inquiry (pp. 101–119). Dewey sought to articulate the essential pattern of knowledge creation in its most general but also most useful and desirable form. He defined the pattern thus: "Inquiry is the controlled or directed transformation of an indeterminate situation into one that is so determinate in its constituent distinctions and relations as to convert the elements of the original situation into a unified whole" (pp. 104–105).

The episode of PBL not only fits but also exemplifies the six characteristics of inquiry that Dewey outlined. First, the situation that the students encounter is problematic; it is unsettled, confusing, and lacking an obvious resolution. Second, the PBL context draws from this situation a definite problem to be resolved—the problem of making a diagnosis. Third, proposals that anticipate solutions are made by the participants, particular examples being the two theories that Betty introduces. Fourth, a process of reasoning intervenes to judge among the alternatives by attending to their networks of meanings. As Dewey (1938) stated:

> Through a series of intermediate meanings, a meaning is finally reached which is more clearly *relevant* to the problem at hand than the originally suggested idea. It indicates operations which can be performed to test its applicability, whereas the original idea is usually too vague to determine crucial operations. In other words, the idea or meaning when developed in discourse directs the activities, which, when executed, provide needed evidential material. (p. 112)

This PBL episode proceeds just so. Fifth, the directed transformation alluded to in Dewey's definition proceeds by an interplay of operations on the empirical and conceptual elements of the situation. The operations on the empirical aspects "bring into high relief conditions previously obscure, and relegate to the background other aspects that were at the outset. The ground and criterion of the execution of this work of emphasis, selection, and arrangement is to delimit the problem" (Dewey, 1938, pp. 117–118). Such is the case with the students' use of the chart to identify the spatial location of the problem-causing brain deformation. Simultaneously, operations on concepts such as TIA (transient ischemic attack) and RIND (reversible ischemic neurological deficit) serve to seek coherence in a network of meanings. The end result is a resolved and settled situation in which the participants agree on the nature of the problem and its description in diagnostic categories. This episode of PBL thus exemplifies Deweyan inquiry.

The reader may have noticed that Dewey gave six characteristics of inquiry, but I have only listed five so far. That is because I find Dewey's discussion of the sixth characteristic troublesome. Fortunately, the sixth characteristic is one of the prime emergent themes of the PBL episode, and therefore, these analyses offer an opportunity for progress. In the remainder of this article, I construct a conversation on this opportunity (although I again emphasize that I am in part putting these analysts up to this job; each can also be read profitably within its own frame of reference).

Dewey's sixth characteristic is that inquiry sits on the boundary between commonsense and scientific reasoning; it is an available tool in both realms, and the prime instrument of the development of the latter from the former. Hall echoes the theme with his paradox: "On one hand, we render the practices of professional 'technoscientists' as being ordinary; on the other hand, we render the practices of people in 'ordinary conversation' as being scientific" (p. 187). Hall labels this a *paradox* because, if our analytic frame eliminates all distinctions between everyday and specialized discourse, it renders meaningless the obvious distinction between a layperson and a professional. However, if our analytical frame renders the distinction too sharply, a great divide (Latour, 1987) is instituted between common sense and science, and an uncrossable gulf disrupts the continuity of development (Smith, diSessa, & Roschelle, 1993–1994).

Dewey never satisfactorily articulated the differences between commonsense and scientific reasoning, and he did not give a genetic developmental account (i.e., Inhelder & Piaget, 1958) of children's learning of specialized technoscientific practices. For example, he distinguished scientific inquiry as being about the relations of meanings, whereas commonsense inquiry is about perceived and enjoyed qualities. This seems to deny nonspecialists the opportunity to enjoy reasoning at the developmental level that Piaget called *formal*—Dewey seemed to insist that people do not think about the coherence of meanings in everyday life. In his historical account of the development of science, technology looms large. Advanced instrumentalities become abstracted from their direct use in everyday life and become appreciated for the ability to further the cause of knowledge for its own sake. (Indeed, the use of video by these analysts fits this model. In the hands of the authors of this special issue, the consumer camcorder designed for enjoying baby pictures and wedding memories is transformed into an instrument of scientific data capture.) However, Dewey does not discuss how ontogenesis recapitulates this bit of phylogenesis; how do learners become proficient in the technologies that support advanced inquiry? These are the challenges I take up in discussing each of the five articles.

ANALYZING THE ANALYTIC ACCOUNTS

To begin, Glenn et al. give an account of the conversational microstructure of the PBL episode. In their account, analytic terms that apply to everyday conversation are shown to also apply to the pragmatics of conversing about a medical "theory." Indeed, the theory is shown to be jointly constructed, the object of what Dewey would call "conjoint activity." A distinguishing feature of scientific (or professional) activity in Dewey's view is that it is more strictly regulated to weed out unwarranted assertions, self-interested points of view, intellectual laziness, received dogmas, and so on (Westbrook, 1991). Although Dewey often alludes to conversation, and shared meaning, he had no tools at his disposal to show in detail how conversation serves to regulate the creation of shared meaning. Glenn et al.'s analysis shows how everyday conversational acts are efficacious tools for regulating a specialized subject matter. Thus, this analysis establishes an important developmental continuity—everyday conversational turn taking is available for regulating medical discourse and, thus, can pragmatically constrain learners' discourse to approximate the norms of the professional culture of medicine. In the PBL setting, the coach and peers may make use of relatively robust and conventional pragmatics to deal with the considerable uncertainties and instabilities in students' medical reasoning capabilities.

Frederiksen's analysis complements Glenn et al.'s by attending to the discourse macrostructure, which Frederiksen characterizes as the diagnostic frame. This frame gives a surprisingly coherent hierarchical account of what appears superficially to be a rambling conversation. Frederiksen points out how the coach orchestrates this conversation to fit this frame with a few well-placed interventions while allowing the students to fill in most of the content. This is interesting because it shows there are two possible framings of the same episode that apply simultaneously but are not necessarily shared. First, as argued earlier, the episode fits the overall pattern of inquiry, which Dewey presumes to be pervasive in successful resolution of indeterminate situations. Second, the episode fits the more technical and specialized pattern of medical diagnosis, which Frederiksen assumes to discriminate doctors from laypeople (at least partially). Is anyone in the episode besides the coach aware of the specialized framing? It is possible that the students are explicitly aware of the pattern of diagnostic reasoning, but it is also possible that they are not and are simply proceeding within the more general pattern of inquiry. The coach could be providing scaffolding to allow general inquiry to be read as diagnosis without the students attending to his moves as such. If the diagnostic procedure is not explicit, we can assume that, sooner or later, the coach will raise the procedure as a topic for reflection or that students will be implicitly conditioned to follow this procedure. Either way, the overlapping frames of inquiry and diagnosis enable learners to participate in a more specialized practice before they fully internalize its nuances. Moreover, the presence of the coach in PBL shapes this transitional practice to move incrementally toward its eventual professional form. Putting these two analyses together reveals everyday patterns in both microstructure and macrostructure that enable the coach and peers to impose regulation on discourse that aids learning.

Frederiksen's approach also contrasts with Dewey's approach (along with many of the other analysts) because of its emphasis on a unifying cognitive theory. Dewey instead grounds his analysis of practice in biological and cultural elements. Mental categories for Dewey can be useful terms of analysis but are not fundamentally explanatory. The cognitive emphasis appears to capture some aspects of this episode while leaving out others. For example, Frederiksen's analysis excels at displaying an invisible deep structure that gives coherence to the overall reasoning process. However, a purely cognitive analysis appears restricted to analyzing relations among already-formed descriptions but misses the problematic interplay between more preconceptual, qualitative experience and theoretically informed discussion (Clancey, 1997). In particular, the bit about locating the categorical brain structures in the unparsed picture of the brain, which looms large in both Hall's and Lemke's account, is seen by Frederiksen as a relatively modular insertion of one pedagogic frame into another. The connection between locating the hippocampus and resolving the diagnostic problem is given short shrift. A similar contrast is found in the analysis of contributions. On a conversational analytic account, a contribution is enacted by a patterned interchange among conversants, leading to acceptance or rejection (Clark & Schaefer, 1989). In Frederiksen's discourse analysis, an utterance with identifiable propositional content is a contribution regardless of its conversational uptake. Overall, Frederiksen seems to assume that cognitive features of this discourse from his point of view (which may be shared with the coach) are available to the medical students as opportunities to further their learning. Under the conversation analysis principle of procedural consequentiality, it would remain to be seen if such features as forward and backward chaining of inferences are actually noticed by students and if they are acted or reflected on.

Palincsar's article begins on a very Deweyan theme, "Discussion in a group does for thinking what testing on real objects does for seeing" (Abercrombie, as cited in Palincsar, p. 161). For Dewey, the hallmark of productive inquiry is its eventual resolution of problems in worldly experience, not just conceptual descriptions. The process of doing experiments and undergoing their consequences is fundamental. Furthermore, in Dewey's account of phylogenesis, experience gradually becomes less directly biological (like seeing) and more culturally mediated (like discussion). Palincsar thus draws attention to an important characteristic of PBL—it offers students a *simulation* of the experience of medical diagnosis, in which discourse substitutes for direct perception of symptoms and readings. Unlike merely reading a text, the discourse situation provides a reactive environment that responds to students' trials and serves as a proxy for experimenting on a real patient. Thus, Betty appears not only to "do" having a theory but also to "undergo" having a theory, as the PBL discourse reacts and holds her accountable to the standards of professional judgment.

The central point of Palincsar's analysis speaks directly to the problem of continuity between commonsense and professional modes of practice. Although we could see the idea of a "transitional community" as a further specification of a Deweyan community of inquiry that bridges everyday and professional practice, Dewey never really gets down to this level of detail. Palincsar uses developmental ideas from Vygotsky, which support a genetic account of the kind Dewey desires but never provides. From Palincsar, we learn that participating in a transitional community of inquiry requires managing the tension between advancing knowledge and maintaining social coherence: "The risk of failure to do this is that students' interpersonal agendas can usurp the problem-solving activity" (p. 166). Just as in Glenn et al.'s and Frederiksen's articles, the issue of proper regulation of professional discourse is made salient. However, in contrast to those articles, Palincsar identifies an everyday skill of self-regulation, the ability to modulate verbal fluency to indicate a self-identity on the boundary between student and professional. It seems plausible that a variety of capacities for self-regulation are essential to successful transition between commonsense and scientific modes of practice.

Lemke picks up another aspect of the interplay at the boundary. Dewey offered a distinction that resembles Lemke's typological–topological distinction, arguing that scientific inquiry is primarily oriented to the quantitative, whereas everyday inquiry is oriented to the qualitative. Dewey's qualitative–quantitative distinction does not seem to be productive for this PBL episode however. The students never engage with the direct qualities of perception (hot–cold, bright–dark, soft–hard, etc.), and quantitative reasoning does not predominate. Moreover, overemphasizing a qualitative–quantitative distinction misses the central role of qualitative reasoning in expert scientific performance (e.g., Forbus, 1984). The typological–topological distinction, however, does play into this PBL episode, yielding the insight that many of the coach's moves press for categorical distinctions, whereas many of the students' moves draw on their resources for making meaning from continuous variation. This suggests that we could safely distinguish professional from everyday practice by attending to its emphasis on greater conceptual precision and accuracy, whether that precision is typological (categorical) or quantitative. At the same time, we could notice that students' significant resources for meaning making often lie in qualitative and topological dimensions. Thus, although precision is a hallmark of professional judgment, the interplay of precise and continuous modes offer students resources for gradually mastering the tools of professional reasoning.

Hall's analysis brings to the foreground two points that further illuminate the theme of inquiry as proceeding at the boundary of common sense and science. First, he draws attention to the role of technologies in making the PBL discussion specialized to medicine in a way the dinner table conversation is not. The chart, he argues, makes a theoretical view of a generalized brain available to the participants, and this is a considerably more refined object than the stuff of dinner table talk. Here, notice that two views of the chart become available. From the viewpoint of the present, the chart serves as a map on which students can trace a path to locate the hippocampus. However, from the viewpoint of the history of technology, the chart serves as a theoretical resource that has been normalized to support reasoning about disease on the basis of location of brain function. These two viewpoints are superimposed through the interplay of ordinary spatial language (*up* and *down*) and professional spatial language (*posterior* and *anterior*). Dewey often referred to inquiry as technological—as essentially an instrumental and instrumented process (Hickman, 1990). Moreover, he viewed scientific inquiry as distinguished from commonsense inquiry partially on the basis of more refined tools. However, Hall's analysis brings forth another point: Technologies can simultaneously be approached from specialized (refined) and ordinary (common) vantage points. Technologies (at least those that are pedagogically useful) serve to bridge ordinary and specialized forms of inquiry by sitting on the boundary.

Second, Hall points out that the students are simultaneously discussing a particular brain and a generalized brain. Of Dewey's various ways of distinguishing the ordinary and the scientific, his emphasis on the generality of the scientific is one of the few that seems compelling. Dewey (1958) described scientific generality in terms of substitution:

> The possibility of regulating the occurrence of any event depends upon the possibility of instituting substitutions. By means of the latter, a thing which is within the grasp is used to stand for another thing, which is not immediately had, or which is beyond control. . . . Modern science is, taken generically, a method of thoroughgoing substitutions. (p. 142)

In Hall's analysis, a substitution of the generic brain (on the chart) for a specific patient's brain (not available) is essential to the progress of this episode of PBL. In contrast, the dinner table conversation is about specific chili peppers, past and present.

CONCLUSIONS

In summary, although the authors of the five articles did not set out to solve a particular problem, their analyses do go quite a distance toward illuminating the relation between ordinary and professional discourse in development. As Hall points out, this relation leads to paradox if analysis renders the participants indistinguishable. The relation also leads to paradox if analysis opens an insurmountable gap between ordinary and specialized forms of participation. Glenn et al. and Frederiksen eliminate part of this paradox by showing how ordinary and professional discourse can coincide and mutually regulate each other, both at the microstructural and macrostructural level. This makes it possible to participate in a professional discourse without already having mastered its specialized forms and, thus, enables learning. Palincsar complements their analysis by showing how students regulate their own discourse to maintain the social cohesiveness of their transitional community. In collaborative learning, both conceptual and social cohesiveness must be managed. Lemke and Hall each help distinguish professional from everyday discourse. Lemke points to the emphasis on precise categories in professional talk, whereas Hall points to their greater generality. Hall also identifies the role of technologies in bringing a history of past inquiry into present learning situations. Both carefully point out that these more professional forms coexist and interact with ordinary forms, thus supporting professional development.

To design and improve learning environments and pedagogical formats, educators need more knowledge of how commonsense and professional discourses coexist, relate, and mutually engage. These five articles show the potential of videotape and multidisciplinary discourse analysis to meet this need. They also exhibit the challenges that lie ahead in bringing such analyses to bear directly on one another.

REFERENCES

Clancey, W. J. (1997). *Situated cognition.* New York: Cambridge University Press.

Clark, H. H., & Schaefer, E. F. (1989). Contributing to discourse. *Cognitive Science, 13,* 259–294.

Dewey, J. (1916). *Democracy and education.* New York: Macmillan.

Dewey, J. (1938). *Logic: The theory of inquiry.* New York: Holt.

Dewey, J. (1958). *Experience and nature.* New York: Dover.

Forbus, K. D. (1984). Qualitative process theory. In D. G. Bobrow (Ed.), *Qualitative reasoning about physical systems* (pp. 85–168). Cambridge, MA: MIT Press.

Hickman, L. A. (1990). *John Dewey's pragmatic technology.* Bloomington: Indiana University Press.

Inhelder, B., & Piaget, J. (1958). *The growth of logical thinking from childhood to adolescence: An essay on the construction of formal operational structures.* London: Routledge.

Latour, B. (1987). *Science in action.* Cambridge, MA: Harvard Univerisity Press.

Schegloff, E. A. (1992). On talk and its institutional occasions. In P. Drew & J. Heritage (Eds.), *Talk at work* (pp. 101–134). Cambridge, England: Cambridge University Press.

Smith, J. P., III, diSessa, A. A., & Roschelle, J. (1993–1994). Misconceptions reconceived: A constructivist analysis of knowledge in transition. *The Journal of the Learning Sciences, 3,* 115–163.

Westbrook, R. B. (1991). *John Dewey and American democracy.* Ithaca, NY: Cornell University Press.

www.ingramcontent.com/pod-product-compliance
Ingram Content Group UK Ltd.
Pitfield, Milton Keynes, MK11 3LW, UK
UKHW020428010325
455677UK00029B/1056